CW00821981

CONTENTS

Acknowledgements

I should like to record my grateful thanks for their help and encouragement with the writing of this book to Mike Leigh, Martin Banham, friends and colleagues in the School of Drama and Theatre Studies at Bretton Hall College – in particular Paul Cowen and Richard Twinem – and to Alan MacDonald and David Farnsworth.

The principal sources for this book are Mike Leigh himself and his work. Any unattributed quotations in the text may be understood to be drawn from innumerable conversations we've had since October 1965 or from a number of taped interviews he was kind enough to allow me to record in November 1980, July 1981 and September 1982. Otherwise, notes of attribution give the appropriate source for all quotations.

INTRODUCTION

I make no claims for this being anything other than a personal book about the work of Mike Leigh. It's work which I have admired since I saw the first play he developed from improvisation in 1965, and while I don't profess to like all his major plays and films equally, my perspective is ultimately that of an enthusiast.

Mike Leigh creates his work through improvisation. The actors invent characters, the characters are put together in improvised situations and out of the material thus created comes, after two and a half months or so, a finished piece of drama. That much is generally known. Although there have been numerous journalistic sketches of his way of working, some more thorough and penetrating than others, there has not yet been any detailed account of the development of his method or any elucidation of the principles on which it's based. The result of these omissions has been, at best, confusion, and, at worst, misunderstanding and misrepresentation. In trying to present as accurate an account as possible of what actually goes on in his rehearsals, I hope to demystify things and to dispose of, I hope for ever, the notion that Leigh casts actors under some sorcerer's spell, or that he bullies them into coming up with what he knew was going to happen all along. He's developed a way of creating the material for drama which allows great creativity and freedom for all concerned. It seems to me that this is something to rejoice in and, if possible, to learn from.

There is another purpose for giving an account of Leigh's working method. Misunderstandings and misrepresentations of his rehearsal practices abound and the debate about how he works has tended to obscure an informed discussion of his plays and films as free-standing artefacts. Perhaps, once an account of the method has been given, public fascination with how he works will give way to an equal fascination with what he has to say to us.

With regard to the discussion of the finished pieces themselves – a discussion which makes up the second half of this book – I find myself on less sure ground. This is a short book, and I'm conscious of having offended against the laws of responsible criticism by having been able to consider only a handful of works in any detail, and even then to have argued general points from particular cases instead of taking each work on its own merits. What I've been concerned to do is to draw the reader's attention to what I think are some of the most important characteristics of Leigh's work as a whole and to suggest ways of looking at his plays and films which might not have been suggested before. The final chapter is not intended to be exhaustive, nor is it meant to serve as any kind of interim assessment. A full and thorough book of that kind still remains to be written. At its simplest, I offer the final chapter as a corrective to the prevailing critical attitude to Leigh's work which until very recently, and with one or two notable exceptions, has covered a pretty narrow spectrum from indifference to outright abuse. I find myself echoing exactly the words of Tony Coult, who in an earlier book in this series, on Edward Bond, justified his own enthusiasm in these terms: 'If I am wrong . . . then at least it can be said that some attempt at balance was made.'

There is a further difficulty inherent in any discussion of Leigh's major work and that is its limited availability. Of the four major stage plays, *Babies Grow Old, Abigail's Party, Ecstasy* and *Goose-Pimples,* only the second and fourth have been published, although a scripted version of *Ecstasy* does exist. Similarly, his work for the cinema and television exists only on film or on videotape. One of the TV plays, *Knock for Knock,* has been inexplicably wiped by the BBC, and his radio play, *Too Much of a Good Thing,* has never been broadcast on the official grounds of its 'banality' although the real reason is obviously attributable to old-fashioned censorship of pre-1968 vintage: there's a sex scene in the play. The problem of this material's not being widely available is compounded by the fact that Leigh's work for the theatre exists in its definitive form in his own productions. Since 'writing' and production aren't two separate processes with him, it's essential that we see performance as part of the substance of the text.

The sum of all these factors is that a fair amount of the final chapter is devoted to describing what actually happens in a particular play or film. I draw some comfort, however, from the fact that in my experience the arrival of a new Mike Leigh play on television is something for an event for a lot of people, and that once seen they're rarely forgotten. 'They're not like what you get on television most of the time,' someone said to me during the writing of this book. 'They're so real. They make you think.'

1: BEGINNINGS

Mike Leigh was born in 1943 in Salford, the son of a doctor, and grew up 'as a middle-class kid right in the middle of a working-class area.' Although he went to the local primary school and later to Salford Grammar School, 'most of my mates were elsewhere; I never used really to play with kids round my way.' Unable, because of 'two left feet', to kick a football, he found a role for himself 'as a sort of resident comedian' to compensate for this shortcoming. He showed a precocious early talent for drawing and would amuse his friends with his caricatures and cartoons of other people. After a grammar school career which was blighted by a complete absence of any disciplined approach to work, he left at the age of seventeen with three O-levels and went, on a scholarship, to RADA with the vague idea that ultimately he wanted to write, direct and make films.

He sees his childhood experiences in Salford, living as a middle-class child in a working-class environment, an outsider in his own neighbourhood, as a significant influence on the themes, ideas and materials throughout his work:

I have got a middle-class background and a completely genuine knowledge about working-class life; there's a kind of ambivalence in my background which is totally genuine. I grew up from the earliest with a consciousness of the existence of class. I think that is an important aspect of what it is I naturally keep saying and looking at.

He had no idea what to expect from RADA but his two years there proved to be 'in the main an extremely sterile experience,' even though it was, in terms of the traditional type of training offered to fledgeling actors, one of the best schools in the country. But Leigh, without really understanding why, found his experience of this type of training, 'ninety-nine per cent dead'.

The business of RADA was (and is) to take talented young people and, by teaching the skills and crafts of the profession, to train them for the stage. The problem which Leigh encountered in 1960 was that the theatre as perceived by RADA was still rooted in a traditional and conservative idea of its nature and purpose. It reflected the values of a West End theatre which Kenneth Tynan described as:

virtually dominated by a ruthless three-power coalition consisting of drawing-room comedy and its junior henchmen, murder melodrama and barrack-room farce. Although competitive among themselves, the members of the combine were united in their determination to prevent the forces of contemporary reality from muscling in on their territory. The average playwright had ceased trying to hold the mirror up to nature, and the fashionable playwright could not possibly hold a mirror up to anything, since genteel idiom demanded the use of the word 'looking-glass'. Nightly, in dozens of theatres, the curtain rose on the same set. French windows were its most prominent feature, backed by a sky-cloth of brilliant and perpetual blue.[1]

Although the then principal of the school, John Fernald, directed productions of Brecht and Chekhov, the main body of the RADA establishment had yet to accommodate the idea of a vital, serviceable and contemporary theatre which was already to be found in much of the new writing and stage experimentation of the time.

In spite of the very obvious differences in content and style, the work of many of the new wave of British dramatists in the late fifties and early sixties shows a common determination to break through the traditional constraints of subject matter, staging and actor/audience relationship which had dominated the theatre since before the second world war. Arnold Wesker sounded one theme of the new writing when he wrote in 1958:

> I want to write my plays not only for the class of people who acknowledge plays to be a legitimate form of expression, but for those to whom the phrase 'form of expression' may mean nothing whatsoever.[2]

In East London Joan Littlewood was developing with her Theatre Workshop company a brawny, rough theatre based on popular, working-class entertainment forms; John Arden's *Serjeant Musgrave's Dance* had been written in the idiom of a folk ballad in an attempt to put the English public back in touch 'with its own poetic traditions';[3] and John Osborne's plays, while conventional in form, were undoubtedly concerned with contemporary personal and social issues expressed in living contemporary language. Harold Pinter's work was less easily associated with any discernible movement, but his enigmatic world of outcasts, fantasists and loners – itself redolent with the influence of Beckett – resonated with the actual texture and feel of everyday life, even though it was represented as a web of failed communication and repressed violence.

These innovations were 'disparaged' at RADA. The school got on with preparing its students to become actors who would get on with the job, working competently with discipline and with the minimum of fuss. The actor was seen as an interpretive instrument, not as the creative participant in the examination of reality. When the time came for the students to play dramatic characters nothing was done to relate the events which an actor might encounter in a play to the events which he might enounter in the course of real life. What was taught was the way in which things might be contrived for the stage. To be fair, within these limitations (limitations which it shared, incidentally, with every other drama school in Britain) the training of actors was undertaken with great professionalism and with appropriate seriousness. There was work on the technical disciplines of acting, on movement and voice, on style and stage technique. There was work, too, on helping the actor to discover and use his own resources in the truthful interpretation of character and role. But all this work, serious as it was in execution and disciplined in approach, was essentially second hand. Although the school prospectus 'paid lip service' to the ideas of Stanislavski, his principles of grounding the life of a stage character in the actor's own first-hand experience and observation of life were never actually explored. There was almost no

1. *A View of the English Stage,* David Poynter, 1975.

2. 'Let Battle Commence', *Encore Magazine* November 1958; from *New Theatre Voices of the Fifties and Sixties,* Marowitz, Milne, Hale Ed., Eyre Methuen, 1965.

3. John Arden, 'Telling a True Tale', *Encore Magazine,* May 1960; *op. cit.*

improvisation at RADA, either in classes or in rehearsals, and when the time came for the student actors to appear in productions the problems they addressed were learning lines, blocking the moves and 'Do I play this part like Gielgud or Albert Finney?'[4] Acting was explored from a philsophical basis which saw it only in relation to itself. The work of RADA occurred in a vacuum of art.

Joan Littlewood's practical work provides an example of a contrasting approach. Writing about her 1956 production of Behan's *The Quare Fellow,* Howard Goorney recalls:

> Rehearsals were well under way before the cast were given scripts or told what part they were playing. They had just to set about creating the atmosphere of prison life, marching round and round the flat roof of the Theatre Royal as prisoners on exercise. The day to day routines were improvised, cleaning out cells, the quick smoke, the furtive conversation, trading tobacco and the boredom and meanness of prison life were evolved. The improvisations had of course been selected by Joan with the script in mind, and when it was finally introduced the situation and the relationships had been well explored.[5]

The first-hand exploration of prison life described here is an example of the way in which Joan Littlewood built into the experience of her actors a specific, personal sense of atmosphere and locale. The work is not about acting as an isolated activity, but acting as a means of investigating a social phenomenon in the real world, in this case a prison. It was precisely this kind of first hand exploration which Leigh didn't find at RADA and was only to discover for himself some years later.

There was one burst of creative work, however, when towards the end of his second year he directed a student-initiated production of Pinter's *The Caretaker,* even though a senior member of the RADA staff had dismissed the play as 'rubbish' and 'a flash in the pan'. Leigh recalls the great lengths to which he went to make sure that the setting and atmosphere of the play were real. 'We dismantled a garden shed from the house I was living in and used it and its contents as the basis of the set.' Similar attention to detail went into getting the sound of water dripping into an on-stage bucket exactly right. 'We built a sort of tower in the wings' from which someone dropped coins into the bucket. Reproducing so perfectly the sound of the water drip was a 'sheer thrill'. Above all, though, there was 'the wallowing glory of putting on a play, right in the middle of RADA, about an arse-scratching tramp and two other blokes in a grotty room.' As well as the inchoate political statement implicit in his deciding to work on a gritty modern play in the first place, the everyday texture and intense characterisation of *The Caretaker* proved to be a source of creative enjoyment and fulfilment. But apart from the experience of this production, he found most of the course at RADA unsatisfying and barren. He couldn't define when he left there in 1962 what it was that had been missing.

A year later, after a short and 'equally sterile' period as an ASM and bit part actor in films, he enrolled in the pre-diploma course at Camberwell Art School. Sitting one day in the life drawing class:

4. Improvisation was so rare at RADA that Leigh remembers clearly the two occasions on which it was used. He had direct experience of it during James Roose-Evan's rehearsals for Camino Real and at another time, in one of Peter Barkworth's celebrated Technique Classes, the group watched two students improvise a scene between man and wife after each of them had been briefed separately.

5. *The Theatre Workshop Story,* Eyre Methuen, 1981.

I suddenly realised what it had been that we hadn't experienced as actors. In the life drawing class there were a dozen or fifteen kids and everyone was making a serious and original investigation into a real experience. Nobody was doing a second-hand rendering of something. I began to think that acting could be creative in the same way that any artist is.

Although he always refers to this moment of illumination at Camberwell as one of the seminal points in the growth of his thinking about his own work, this awareness of what was wrong, for him, with most acting couldn't be examined at the time through any practical expression of his own. It was his ambition to write, direct, to design and to make films, and he continued his education by studying in the Theatre Design Department at the Central School of Arts and Crafts. He studied too, at the London Film School.

The ideas that acting could be creative and that theatre 'could be made as much a direct expression of one's care about things as could other sorts of art' were stimulated and nourished by the particularly rich cultural atmosphere of the late nineteen-fifties and the early and middle years of the sixties. In drawing attention to some of the things which were in the air during this period, there's no suggestion that Leigh directly absorbed any single influence which can be found reproduced intact in his own work. Then, as now, his way of going about things was particular and idiosyncratic. But like most intelligent young people he simply took in what was going on and used it to sharpen and define his own way of thinking.

In the cinema, which Leigh attended avidly, a new generation of European and Asian films had blown away the rather flat conventions of the narrative-enslaved English and Hollywood cinema. The work of Godard and Renoir, Satyajit Ray, Andrzej Wajda and Yasujiro Ozu (to name but a few) seemed to expand the idea of what a film could be and what the cinema could do. The British film industry had even been prodded into a grittier and more realistic exploration of contemporary life and had brought to prominence a fresh crop of lively young regional actors. From America, in 1960, came John Cassavetes' first film, *Shadows,* which was running in London when Leigh arrived there. 'What one knew about it was that it was improvised.' He remembers it as 'the most specific thing' he was aware of to do with improvisation. If he wasn't fully aware of the *auteur* theory, he had nevertheless realised that in practical terms 'the French film directors had their own films, they were the authors of their own films'.

In addition to the new writers already referred to who, in Tynan's phrase, were making the 'assault on the West End', the theatre was beginning to show other signs of innovation. Peter Hall had become artistic director of the RSC in 1960 at the age of 29. His adaptations of certain European models of policy and practice, most notably the inspiration of the Berliner Ensemble, created an artistically corporate theatre enterprise in which Shakespeare and other classics were produced not as museum exhibits exhumed as a matter of cultural duty, but as works with a currency and relevance to contemporary life. Hall's epic production of Shakespeare's histories in 1963, under the title *The Wars of the Roses,* brought to the establishment theatre many Brechtian values. The unfolding chronicle revealed on stage a brutal struggle for power among real men. This was no celebration of English history in bright armour and ermine, but an exposure of its political mechanism in sweat and iron. One of the most remarkable features of *The Wars of the Roses* was John Bury's design. In 1963 the impact was almost shocking to see on stage clothes, furniture, weapons and utensils which looked as though they had actually been used. Leigh remembers seeing the plays and noticing that 'what was extraordinary was the sense of things being real'.

A contemporary approach to classic texts was not Hall's only innovation. In 1962 he brought into the RSC two of Europe's most original theatre practitioners, Michel St Denis and Peter Brook. Brook's epoch-making production of *King Lear* in 1962 fed into his exploration (with Charles Marowitz) of Artaud's ideas in the Theatre of Cruelty season at LAMDA the following year, which itself culminated in Brook's 1964 production of Weiss's *Marat-Sade*. Leigh saw all this work. Searching for a style of acting which would do away with the phoneyness in the performer, Brook had his actors base their characterisations of the mental patients in the *Marat-Sade* on actual case histories, and they researched for their parts by visiting mental hospitals and talking to psychiatrists. Some of the rehearsal work was recorded for a 1964 BBC TV arts programme, *Omnibus*. Leigh saw the broadcast and remembers thinking, 'if they can do all that, why don't they take it one stage further and make up a play?'

In 1965, he formed with David Halliwell, with whom he'd been friends since RADA, a production company to produce Halliwell's play, *Little Malcolm and his Struggle Against the Eunuchs,* at the Unity Theatre. The six-and-a-half hour script proved intransigent; Leigh directed, but rehearsals, with Halliwell himself playing the central role of Malcolm Scrawdyke, were 'a nightmare'; making all 'the mistakes of a novice' he 'turned in the worst production ever', and the company which had been formed to produce the play, Dramagraph, wound up its affairs profoundly in the red. *Little Malcolm* might seem very much in the mood of the 1960s with its student revolutionaries planning an art school rebellion in Huddersfield, but the point of the play isn't political at all. Scrawdyke is an isolated fantasist, the revolution merely a projection of his mind to conceal his personal inadequacies. For much of the time the play concentrates on his lone figure, cut off from the world around him and talking to himself in soliloquies of self-recrimination and disgust. Although the play is saturated in the idioms of West Yorkshire, Scrawdyke's dramatic antecedents are Winnie, Krapp and Hamm, the similarly isolated soliloquists from the plays of Samuel Beckett.

Before Beckett 'there had of course been . . . attempts to dispense with bourgeois theatrical conventions regarding action'[6] but no one until Beckett had compelled an audience quite so remorselessly to share his characters' time. In the frame of Beckett's stage, unencumbered by the qualities usually associated with entertainment, the most extraordinary things had begun to occur. Since virtually nothing of any great importance seemed to happen to the characters in Beckett's plays, paradoxically everything they did became interesting. Their words appeared to acquire the status of poetry, their movements, the condition of dance. It became a theatre not of 'What happens next?' but of 'What's happening now?'

As well as absorbing all this breaking of new ground in the arts, Leigh was young at a time when being young was beginning to seem less and less of an inhibition to finding a public forum in which to express one's ideas. While the late fifties/early sixties saw nothing so apparently momentous as the radical explosion among young people of 1968, this period did see them asserting their independence of their parents' generation and values. The popular labels of Youth Culture and the Generation Gap which were part of the jargon of these years marked the growing consciousness of a phenomenon which is nowadays so commonplace that to label it as anything would appear eccentric. The great CND rallies and marches of the time appeared to be as much celebrations of youth as they were social protests against nuclear weapons. In an expression of their revulsion at what they saw as the creeping corruption of the

6. Alain Robbe-Grillet, 'Samuel Beckett, or "Presence" in the Theatre', *Samuel Beckett,* Martin Esslin Ed., Prentice-Hall (Spectrum Books), 1965.

materialism of post-war prosperity, many middle-class young people of a left-wing orientation cultivated a deliberately unkempt appearance and put on the radical uniform of duffle coat and sandals. They found their own real values in the American beat poets, traditional and modern jazz and in folk music. The popular press called them Beatniks. It stuck and gave them an identity: unorthodox, caring, articulate and passionately concerned with 'issues'. Knocking around with this crowd by night and attending classes at RADA by day, it is small wonder that Leigh describes his experience of those two years at drama school as 'almost schizophrenic'.

He emerged from the experience of *Little Malcolm* torn between the feelings of 'not being able to direct', and wanting to write his own plays. At the time he saw his future as a writer in fairly conventional terms; writing would be a solitary activity and his idea of the kind of plays he would write was very much influenced by Halliwell's work in the line of Beckett. In fact the first half dozen plays he made out of improvisation show this influence very clearly since part of their dramatic currency was an exploration of the tension between everyday events in the characters' exterior lives and their secret, unfulfilled wishes and dreams in their interior worlds. Jane, for example, the central character in *My Parents Have Gone to Carlisle,* throws a party for her schoolfriends while her parents are away. She resorts to fantasy whenever things get out of hand: thus, although her party turns into an ugly disaster with adolescent high jinks giving way to cruelty and unpleasantness, once the guests have gone she rehearses 'the way she will describe to her parents what a wonderful party it was'. Similarly, Gerald, the central character of *NENAA*, works at a dreary job in a café in King's Cross. Whenever he's alone however he indulges in fantasies 'about founding a North-East New Arts Association – *NENAA* – back home' on Tyneside. He's very vague about the precise nature of the organisation but is inspired both by the word *NENAA* itself, 'which he writes in salt on the tables' and 'by the inevitable possibility of enlisting the secretarial services of one Vera Cudden, who works at the Marley Tiles factory'. Eventually, Gerald is sacked when the café owner finds him 'undressing' Vera on one of the café tables. As well as Gerald's fantasies, the play features the fantasies of the regular café customers which are counterpointed with his.

Although between 1965 and 1969 Leigh created no fewer than nine plays which originated from improvisation, it was not until 1969 that the idea that he would be a solitary writer was 'finally eroded' and he 'absolutely realised' that he 'was not going to sit down alone in a room and write plays', even though he had discovered by the end of 1965 that working through improvisation 'was a way of being a dramatist'.[7]

In 1965 he went as an assistant theatre director to The Midlands Arts Centre and was given the job of initiating drama activities with the large number of young people who had joined the recently opened complex. Since those days it's become commonplace for youth theatres to develop their own work through improvisation, but in 1965 it was a bold and unusual step. The result of the work was *The Box Play*:

> a family of six live in a large cage-like box in the middle of the stage. I decided before work began on the basic theatrical image of the box. This had been suggested to me by a house my sister had just bought on the eve of her marriage. When rehearsals began, I dictated to each actor what his part would be.[8]

7. Only one play written by Leigh has been performed: *Waste Paper Guards,* produced by the Independent Theatre Company in Birmingham in September 1966. The cast was Gillian Trethowan, Les Blair and Paul Clements. Blair also directed.

The manner in which the parts were dictated to the young actors he describes as 'you're the dog; you're the dad; you're the mum – improvise'. Once the parts had been distributed – and parts were created for anyone who came to rehearsals – there followed 'dozens of brief improvisations in which we created, at a very superficial level, the relationships and problems of the characters'. Some of the improvisations were about little more than the generation of dialogue. In one scene an old man who said nothing was pushed about in his wheelchair by a pretty young nurse who chatted gaily about all the beautiful things there were to see in the park. In rehearsal the actress frequently found it difficult to think of anything to say. 'Tell him about the trees', Leigh would suggest. She'd say a few words about the trees. 'There's a bird up there, tell him about that.' She'd say a few words about that. 'Tell him . . .' He later described *The Box Play* as 'force-bred'.

All the improvisations took place under 'normal' rehearsal conditions – that is, the actors not actually working stayed in to watch, and there was no improvisation or paper work concerning the characters' backgrounds or life outside the immediate context of the play . . .
   In the finished production, the acting style, the almost naive content and the design style worked at a superficial caricature level and slapstick and other easy theatrical devices abounded.[8]

Omitted from Leigh's own account is the fact that *The Box Play* was a quite remarkable piece of work in its time and context. It had steered well clear of 'the easy pitfalls of amateur dramatics' and the young performers worked with ease and confidence and a great sense of fun. It *was* very funny in its use of 'easy theatrical devices' and had given the actors the satisfaction of having, in part, created their own play. More than this, as a theatrical cartoon, it worked superbly with its bright, hard, polished surface and it felt very much of its time, for in 1965 we were in the throes of the theatre of the absurd, when plays about dotty families who lived in boxes seemed in no way unusual.
   There followed a couple more cartoon workshops which were never developed into plays for public presentation. Each of them involved a large group of young actors and each consisted of a series of improvisations around a central jokey situation: the attempts of various people to persuade an unseen character to come down from his tower made up the content of the first, and the second concerned fourteen girls, all of them called Doreen, who lived on an island. Dissatisfied with the shallowness of the actors' work, Leigh realised that these workshop projects had taught him a valuable lesson. Making plays 'wasn't all about stringing together vague, superficial theatrical ideas . . . you can't make plays about boxes, islands and towers.' Plays for him, 'whether written or improvised, must be about people and relationships'. If there was to be a development in the content of the plays away from abstracted cartoon representations of reality into something which made possible the exploration of people and relationships, a new method of rehearsal would have to be found. 'You're the dog; you're the dad; you're the mum – improvise' wouldn't do.
   His next play, *My Parents Have Gone to Carlisle,* marks an immense step forward in his method. To begin with, there was no dictating to the young actors who they were going to play. He began this time with no more than an event which they were going to explore: a teenagers' party. And instead of the dozens of brief

8. Mike Leigh, *An Account of the Development of My Improvised Plays 1965-69, An Application for the George Devine Award, 1969.* October 1969.

improvisations of *The Box Play* rehearsals, which yielded shallow caricatures and lots of little scenes with the consistency of jokes, the improvisations for this play –

> were much longer and more detailed and for the first time I realised the importance of having no 'audience' watching the rehearsals apart from myself. This removed the actor's inevitable tendencies towards making unnecessary concessions to 'performing' before the ripe time.[8]

The young nurse from *The Box Play* would have been a lot happier in this rehearsal atmosphere.

> I . . . began to learn that if the actors were to develop their characters and relationships to a state of fluency, and if the improvisations were to be rich enough for me to draw the play from 'real' events, I must sit quietly and patiently for as long as possible, only intercepting when a little guidance was necessary.[8]

These discoveries have since solidified into principles which underpin all his work. The 'real' events he refers to here are, of course, events which become real in the fictional lives of the fictional characters. He discovered that the fuller this fiction becomes, the more packed with biography, past events and relationships, the richer the actual world of the play and the more dense the play's present tense in performance. Pursuing this, he began in the course of these rehearsals to explore the emerging characters in other contexts, finding a life for them beyond the situation which had been originally posited – the party.

When the time came to suspend the improvisations and to assemble the play, he experienced a sensation which is now familiar – a sense of 'complete panic'. Rehearsals had indeed generated plenty of rich material: deep characterisations and dramatic conflicts. But all this material had been developed almost at the expense of its capacity to communicate itself to an audience. It had become difficult 'to bridge the gap between totally realistic improvisations, often introspective and inaudible, and the organised theatrical requirements of the play'. In performance, any panic which had infected the stage at which the play was put together was completely invisible to the audience. It remains in my memory as one of the most impressive pieces of theatrical work by young people I've seen. The performances were deep and alive; the play was well structured and tightly organised and the production perfectly clear in form and meaning.

For Leigh, however, the organisation of the play's surface in performance had been achieved by means which were 'over-technical'. In the interests of performance he had dictated 'moves, rhythms, timing, content to the actors' and in so doing had imposed upon the rehearsal work qualities it had not possessed. A series of rambling, naturalistic improvisations with their own texture and their own sense of reality were transformed by the imposition of performance disciplines into a play, the surface of which was held together by a number of 'cinematic' techniques – jump-cuts, blackouts and shifts of point of view.[9] Furthermore, to create the play's structure he had caused things to happen which did not arise from the characters' motivation.

It was to be some time before he could address this problem again and begin to look

---

9.   The setting of *My Parents Have Gone to Carlisle* was suggested by the minimum of furniture. Jane's house, in which the party was held, was merely a sofa, centre stage. In one memorably cinematic scene there was a brief blackout during which the sofa was reversed and the actors changed their positions in relation to it. When the lights came back the room was now viewed by the audience 'from behind'. This was a brilliant stroke of theatrical inventiveness, but it had nothing whatever to do with the intense naturalism of the rehearsals.

for a way of building into the actors' improvisations work which would allow the structure and conventions of performance to grow organically. It was not until the following year, when he joined the RSC as an assistant director, that he made another improvised play, *NENAA*, this time with professional actors. The problem of how to develop plays organically, he saw, had more ramifications than simply the sense of unease at changing gear from the conventions of improvisation to the conventions of performance:

> I realised that if an improvised play was really to be a totally organic entity, genuinely evolved from characters and relationships, then I had been wrong in starting rehearsals . . . by stating plot or theme and then 'filling it in' . . . I saw that we must start off with a collection of totally unrelated characters (each one the specific creation of its actor) and then go through a process in which I must cause them to meet each other and build a network of real relationships; the play would have to be drawn from the results.[10]

With *NENAA* –

> I wanted to create a play which on the surface looked at very real characters in a real environment, but which would extend, as it developed, into an exploration of the relationship between the everyday hum-drum and these people's fantasies and inner thoughts lurking below the surface.[10]

In place of the 'plot or theme' of the earlier plays there is in this statement something much closer to the 'notion' of which he speaks as the starting point for some of the later plays.

To facilitate the actors' begining work on their individual characterisations he filled the rehearsal room with receptacles – 'boxes, suitcases, egg-cups, a bucket, a coffin etc'. He asked 'each actor to pick one' and then 'to build some character suggested by the object'. The actors worked individually all over the room on the process of character building.

> To get into this character he must talk to himself, making no concessions to performing, and only allow his talk to evolve naturally, in gear with the evolution of his character, rather than allow himself to manufacture dialogue.[10]

When the characters had been created and had reached a state of fluency each actor was asked 'to extend his thought stream to his character's dreams, fantasies or memories'. Thus the inner lives of the characters were created and expressed by means of soliloquy. The 'everyday hum-drum' grew from Leigh's 'creating mutual situations in which groups of first two, then three and later more characters could get to know each other, and build their relationships.'

The subsequent building and structuring of *NENAA* provided an abundance of experiences from which he was to learn a great deal which would inform his work later on. To begin with, the initial stimulus of the receptacles brought forth a far greater range of characters then he had had to deal with before. The young actors at the Midland Arts Centre had made characters with in-built limitations. The homogeneity of *The Box Play* characters was guaranteed because the parts were dictated by Leigh; similarly, the teenagers' party of *My Parents Have Gone to Carlisle* itself determined the kind of people who would attend it. The homogeneity was further reinforced by the similarity of age and background of the actors. 'There was no risk of any of the

10. Mike Leigh, *op. cit.*

characters being outrageous or far-fetched because they were working from that immediate culture that they knew.' But with *NENAA* not only were the actors experienced professionals, they also came from a variety of life experiences. 'The scale of the thing was huge.' Twelve characters, with little in common, had to be accommodated in some way.

> I had recognised in the character Gerald a potential protagonist . . . but . . . I couldn't yet see how I was to resolve this particular Tyneside lad, working as a filing clerk in London, with, say, an Italian barber, a dustman, a garage attendant and a baker's apprentice.[10]

The holding form of the play was discovered when the actor playing the barber asked if his character could become, instead, a café proprietor. In the creation of the café there developed a world which could hold the range of the characters together and still allow Gerald to be the play's protagonist. 'Remaining the same character, but changing his job . . . Gerald went to work in the (ex-barber's) café.

Presented in these simple terms and with the omniscience of hindsight the way in which the play found its form appears self-evident, but these adjustments, necessitated by the range of work which had been developed, contained an important discovery:

> What we are in life may be conditioned by what we do or by the role circumstances force us to play, but this is not necessarily the case, and we would remain our inherent selves irrespective of job or role.[10]

In other words a character may be built upon a specific foundation but will embody two qualitatively different strands: his material circumstances and his inherent self. The inherent self is not necessarily compromised by changes in material circumstances. This discovery has been crucially important in Leigh's work ever since, for it has become one of the devices through which he has been able to control the composition of his plays, moving characters into and out of marriages, jobs and professions, for example.

There is even more to it than that. In the very process of adjusting the material circumstances of a character a fuller biography is created. Gerald's change of job, for example, was accomplished by 'creating the fact that on leaving the office he decided to try something different'. In other cases changes in circumstances can be improvised and built solidly into the character's actual experience as real events. In yet other cases changes may simply occur as a matter of agreement.

One of the results of this discovery was the compositional freedom which it bestowed, Leigh had found a way of shaping plays by being able to move characters into relationships and situations which carried implications for the form of the finished piece. But the discovery embodied, too, another dramatic possibility which went beyond this formal, compositional aspect. By moving characters through and by investigating a number of jobs, relationships or other social circumstances, each of which contributes to the living bulk of the character's memory of his own past, there is a tension created between the character's previous experience and his perceptions and behaviour in the present tense.

Leigh found, as well, that the very circuitousness of the route by which a character arrives at the destination of what he is in the final play contributes directly to the play's density of texture:

> Had I started out by simply saying, 'Let's do a play set in a café', not only would that have been a thoroughly arbitrary choice in the context of my primary objectives,

but of greater importance is that the actors would have put the cart before the horse, conceiving the characters as café customers rather than as people with a wider reality.[10]

In one improvisation, Gerald, still a filing clerk, had had his hair cut by the barber. When Gerald came to work in the café, the barber shop improvisation had 'laid the foundations for a far more interesting relationship than the previous employer-employee conflict we would have arrived at had we not got to the thing so circuitously'.

In the work on *NENAA* Leigh drew together a large number of the threads which had been left dangling from the earlier plays. By modifications and developments in his rehearsal procedures and by his recognition of the flexibility which the work could achieve he had acquired, as a director, a new set of skills which, in turn, made accessible richer areas of content. The play was a great success at its performance in the RSC studio at Stratford. In spite of this he still felt that he hadn't got it right; that there was further to go. The way the characters had been made 'left a great deal to be desired'. They 'had grown into quite real people' but 'still lacked a certain dimension.'

When, in 1969, he was able to describe in detail the way of working which he had evolved, Leigh wrote:

> Ethically, I prefer to draw from actual specific experience rather than from woolly generalised notions . . . The more a dramatist draws from specific experience, the richer the content . . .[10]

While the characters in *NENAA* had become 'quite real' they had not been created from specific experience. The receptacles had served to 'get the ball rolling' but had inevitably set the actors working in a generalised way. For example, the actor who began with the brief-case was instantly taken into thinking of the types of people who might carry a brief-case – 'businessman', 'school teacher' or 'office worker'. For the actor who picked the dustbin, 'dustman' was about his only choice. At risk of belabouring a simple point, there is a world of difference between 'dustman' expressed as a general type, and 'a particular dustman I know' as a specific individual. Whereas 'dustman type' will bring stereotypes flooding into the mind which are unlikely to vary much from person to person (notions such as 'working-class', 'burly'), 'a particular dustman I know' is instantly more interesting because specific and personal. It is also possible to describe the latter from objective and detailed observation of actual experience.

The task confronting the cast of *NENAA* was to work up a specific character from the generalisation of the stimulus. The stimulus of the receptacles was useful to a degree. It produced a wide range of individual characters and the receptacles themselves, contemporary objects suggesting an everyday function, served to imply the social territory of the play. But, more subtly, this stimulus set the actors going in a way which actually cut across the way Leigh discovered he wanted to work. The dimension the characters lacked was particularity. Leigh's judgement on *NENAA* was that there had been a shortfall between his objectives for the play and what had finally been performed – the difference between the 'very real' characters he wanted and the 'quite real' people he got; and that this shortfall was attributable to the starting point.

He perceived that if, as a dramatist, he was genuinely to be in control of the material, he must get in on the ground floor of character-making and share that work *with* the actor instead of abdicating it *to* the actor and confining his function to an orchestration of what the actor comes up with. Furthermore, in order to make the plays with that intense particularity which is now one of the hallmarks of his style, there had to be a coherent and organic connection between the point at which work on the play began and the point at which it finished, between the first rehearsal and the last performance. Apart from anything else, beginning with receptacles was inadequate 'because they had nothing to do with the final play'.

'Seek your examples in life,' Shtchepkin taught his pupils. And to the actor, Shumsky, he wrote:

> Always have nature before your eyes; enter so to say, into the skin of the role you are playing, study well its social locale, its education, its peculiar ideas if they are present, and do not forget to study its past life.[11]

As if following this advice, Leigh began to work on his next improvised play, *Individual Fruit Pies,* made with students at the E15 Acting School, in a new and quite particular way:

> For the first time I made a definite decision about what I was concerned with and I quite specifically said to the actors: 'I want you to think of someone you know, a real person, who could be in a bed-sitter.'[11]

It's important to stress that the decision to have the actors base their characters on a real life model wasn't simply an arbitrary substitute for the receptacles of *NENAA* or the party theme of *My Parents Have Gone to Carlisle.* Nor was it just a different method of starting rehearsals which happened to work. It was a decision made after conscious reflection on what he saw as the shortcomings of his work to date. He had no way of knowing at the time that it was going to work better than the other starting points, nor did he have a premonition that it was to be the foundation upon which all his plays were subsequently to be built. What this new basis for the work did offer was a means of creating great freedom for the actor, with the insurance that Leigh himself sought as a director, that he could share in and control the creative process of character making at the most fundamental level.

The use of the word 'control' in this context, with its unfortunate associations of imposed disciplines, might be more than a little misleading if it suggests a director, iron-clad and ferocious, wrestling with the will of the wayward actor and interfering with his best efforts. As with any good director, Leigh's method of conducting rehearsals is more to do with the structuring of creative opportunities for actors than with their propulsion towards a predetermined destination. The actor's work is controlled, certainly, within the boundaries suggested by the slowly-emerging play, but within these obvious limits, and the increasingly specific demands which they inevitably entail, the actor has great freedom.

In his rehearsals for *Individual Fruit Pies* Leigh –

> . . . went much further than (he) had done previously in the use of a complete series of improvisations which did not finally appear in the play, but which created a totally realistic background of experience for each character.[12]

For example, one of the characters, a bed-ridden old lady, is visited each Sunday by her nephew and niece:

11. Constantin Stanislavski, *My Life in Art,* Trans. J. J. Robbins, Eyre Methuen, 1980.

12. Mike Leigh, *op. cit.*

The old woman's fading recognition of her nephew and niece could only work so accurately because we had spent two days on a series of improvisations about those characters twenty, fifteen, ten and five years previously.[12]

Such work as this was, in part, a consequence of the intense individuality of the characterisations. A great degree of thoroughness was called for in investing these characters with a coherent theatrical life – a theatrical life which would be commensurate in its own reality with the detailed observation and specificity on which the characters were based.

The actors' use of real models for their characters 'worked magnificently' and led to the making of 'the first, proper, actual play' with a wide range of authentic characters:

... had *Individual Fruit Pies* ... begun with the actors being themselves, or with their using inanimate objects, I could never in ten centuries have had somebody come up with a shrewdly-observed mongol like the one we had.[11]

The reality and depth of these characterisations called for a more rigorous set of rehearsal conventions. Investigations of characters' backgrounds occurred within a strict discipline of chronology so that the past life of a character accumulated in an orderly and coherent way. Similarly, the creation of the actual world of the rooming house and the network of relationships within it involved the actor in stiffer conventions of sustaining improvisations and remaining in character for extended periods. Some of the play's action, however, derived from a more schematic mode of working. In one scene, for example, Ron, the central character, and an office girl, one of the tenants, 'indulge in a joint fantasy in which she pretends he is her baby'. During the rehearsals, the office girl developed an obsession for the baby of one of the other tenants. The background for her obsession

... evolved through her baby-sitting seven or eight times. But a new level of reality was reached when I got her to imagine the baby was Ron, and then got Ron into the rehearsal and asked her to talk to him as if he were a baby. This, plus his response to this behaviour, gave us a scene for the play which we could not have arrived at directly, and which was, thus, theatrical and dramatic, whilst remaining real for the actors.[12]

What emerges from this account is that while the actor's work must be based in the reality of the character's world, situations may be contrived which throw together these worlds in unexpected combinations to produce extraordinary new planes of experience for the character and new insights for the actor.

To the discovery made during the work on *NENAA,* that a character's inherent self can remain the same whatever his material circumstances, was added this new awareness that as long as improvisation is based on circumstances which are real for the character he can be taken into areas of himself and his relationships with others which are unexpected and startling. This, too, was an important discovery for the flexibility it allowed in the composition of the plays; it made possible not only the moving of characters in and out of jobs and marriages etc, but also the exploration and representation of areas of the character's self which, in the normal run of things, would be only vaguely implied. To put it plainly, Ron's participation in the baby fantasy was an expression of a part of himself which it took the actual situation to bring out. By working beneath the surface of a character's behaviour, by exploring the ways he would behave in a situation which, in the course of his everyday life he would be unlikely to encounter, Leigh is able to define the remoter areas of human behaviour.

The work which went into the making of *Individual Fruit Pies* 'has been the basis of my approach on all the improvised plays since'. The development of the method over these four plays is essentially the story of the work of an artist to master his medium. Leigh had discovered that in improvisation he had a plastic medium, with its own disciplines and techniques, through which he could define those areas of life about which he cared with as much precision and exactness as a writer working alone in the study. Furthermore, since the very substance of the medium is character and behaviour, he could explore regions of human interaction and social territory which resist definition in words.

In the 1982 BBC TV documentary, *Mike Leigh Making Plays*, Leigh worked with Sam Kelly, Alison Steadman and David Threlfall for the purpose of demonstrating the way his method works. It's important to emphasise that the work shown in this film was strictly and solely for the purposes of demonstration and that there was no intention to create a serious play. Leigh and the actors created three characters who were themselves theatre people engaged in the process of trying to make an improvised play. The director of the piece, Mick Leeming, is a self-regarding and entirely vague individual whose idea of work is to release a torrent of freely associated ideas without ever alighting on a single specific thought or concrete task for his actors. His rehearsals quickly degenerate into an anarchic, self-indulgent free-for-all. While Leeming flits about pursuing his elusive brainstorms, the actress, Miranda, suggests with growing exasperation exercises and activities which they might do to get something started and Merton Savoy, a middle-aged mediocre rep actor of the old school, struts around clutching his brief case without a clue as to what's going on. At one point he asks Leeming what sort of character Leeming wants him to play; 'You are man, you are life, go with it.' is the reply.

In this demonstration Leigh is obviously spoofing some of the wilder ideas which people have about his own work. But for all their absurdity Leeming's rehearsals are a parody of a sort of artiness for which Leigh has never had any time. Leeming is concerned with vague and undelineated notions of creativity but not with life. Miranda is almost as bad. While her suggestions are at least specific, her interests are mostly in the inner psychic energies of acting. In his own way Savoy is a spokesman for the other end of the arty spectrum in the theatre. When he makes his suggestions as to the kind of characters he might play, he offers only stock types from thrillers and drawing-room comedies. Leigh's work has never been in the arty area. He's not interested in exploring the phenomenon of acting for its own sake; he's fascinated neither by the idea of creativity nor by the pushing back of the boundaries of theatrical form. His starting point has always been ordinary life. Even his first play, self-consciously 'stylish' as it was, grew from his thinking about specific experience and developed into the image of people living in a little box cut off from the currents of life which flowed around them.

Nevertheless, his work, particularly in the 1960s, but even today, has been associated with what he himself calls 'the arty-farty experimental kind of director's theatre' which is derided in Leeming's rehearsals. When, in the late sixties and early seventies, he tried to explain his way of working and his purposes, people would usually see what he did either in terms of educational activity or of Happenings and other such spontaneous events. In 1970 he persuaded Charles Marowitz to let him develop a play at the Open Space Theatre. The finished production was the stage version of *Bleak Moments*. Marowitz found the play 'absolutely worthless. Tea, coffee, sherry – improvisation stopped being about that fifteen years ago.' One suspects that this judgment was based on Marowitz's disappointment that *Bleak*

Moments, in that it was about real behaviour in everyday life, had failed to display any experimental credentials. In his review of the play in The Times, Irving Wardle found otherwise. Under the heading 'Embarrassed Actors', Wardle specifically identified the play as 'experimental theatre' and discussed at some length the consequences of the actors having been asked 'to come on cold and improvise a play . . . left entirely to their own resources . . . without the protection of an author or animating director.' The play of *Bleak Moments* was of course as definitively 'scripted' and tightly structured as any of Leigh's work, and to be fair to Irving Wardle, he did later publicly acknowledge that he had been in error in his assessment of the play as as spontaneous, unrehearsed event. As the later film shows, it was because the performances were so real that Wardle thought he was watching actual as opposed to acted embarrassment, and that Marowitz dismissed it in terms of 'naive slice-of-life naturalism' which had no place 'in the post-Artaudian age'.

In spite of their polarity – 'not experimental enough' versus 'too experimental' – these responses to *Bleak Moments* serve as a means to measure the climate of attitudes to experimental work which was the context within which many of Leigh's earlier plays were received. But the fact is that his work was not (and is not) experimental at all in any self-conscious sense. His innovations were not primarily to do with the nature or form of the theatre, but with the content of the material he was working on.

The important distinction to grasp here is that Leigh is not an interpretative director; he's a dramatist who applies the skills of directing, first learned in the 60s and subsequently constantly refined, to the definition of his preoccupations and ideas as an artist. It's extremely misleading to lump his work together with that of those directors – experimental or otherwise – who have used improvisation in their own interpretative work.

Leigh is often asked whether he would direct a scripted play. It's a question to which he frequently gives 'the perverse answer' that he's not a director and isn't interested in directing. The more appropriate question would obviously be whether he'd ever consider taking up his pen to write a play. While it's not my purpose to speculate in such matters, the next chapter will look in some detail at Leigh's work as a dramatist in relation to his skills as a director of actors.

2:THE METHOD

Let's begin with a caveat.

In describing the way in which Leigh works with actors to create plays and films the last thing I want to suggest is that he operates a system. As he has said, 'the time is spent differently on every project', and it would be entirely wrong for anyone to get the idea that he always works in exactly the same way or always does exactly the same things in rehearsal: 'There are as many different kinds of rehearsal exercises and short cuts as there are characters', and all that can be said of them is that 'they all illustrate one fundamental principle or another.' This chapter, then, is about the principles which underpin his work and these principles will be illustrated, where appropriate, by examples from his practice.

The work begins with the selection of the actors. Up to and including the stage version of *Bleak Moments,* Leigh would work with anyone who was willing to do a play with him – 'they were doing me a favour'. Since then he has become increasingly selective in his casting and thorough in his auditioning. This increasing selectivity has undoubtedly contributed to some of the mystique which surrounds his work, but the reasons for it are plain to see in the light of what has already been discussed: since the earliest days he has been working towards the total control of his medium in order to refine the artistic statement. The matter of correct casting is obviously crucial to this control, because there is no role to fall back on, no part requiring an actor of 'appropriate' qualities. As he says, 'It's a rigorous and strict business casting these things.' The criteria he applies to the choice of actors are partly practical, partly philosophical.

Although the work itself is going to be entirely specific and concrete, getting going on a Leigh play involves a great leap in the dark. There has to be, therefore, complete trust between actor and director: trust that the actor is going to be able to create a substantial character guided by Leigh's ground rules; trust that the director is going to be able to develop the material into a finished piece.

The philosophy of the work is that the play is going to involve the investigation of a real world. The character whom the actor will create will be drawn from 'a specific, placeable, social, educational, economic, cultural environment'. Actors who aren't interested in developing characters from this basis are obviously not going to suit Leigh's purposes, nor, it must be said, will he suit theirs, even though these actors 'may be very good in other contexts'.

The fact that Leigh insists that the characters are precisely identifiable in terms of their social/cultural background implies an acknowledgement of the existence of social class. And indeed social class is always part of the very fabric of his plays and films. An actor, therefore, who says, 'Well, I don't really believe in class. I think we're all equal really', is not going to be someone who Leigh will get on with in a professional context.

Another important quality he's looking for in actors is their capacity to be objective about their characters, an ability to regard the character as a third person creation as opposed to a first person manifestation of the actor's self. From a very early stage of rehearsal characters are referred to by both Leigh and the actors as 'He' or 'She', and an objective stance is taken to their actions and behaviour.

Leigh has found that the people with whom he works best, and who work best with him, are 'good, experienced all-round professional character actors, tough-minded and individualistic'. It will be clear, simply from glancing through the cast lists at the end of this book, that Leigh doesn't work with those actors who, for whatever reason, always play a version of themselves or who have become typecast, no matter how subtly, into playing always the same kind of personality. The qualities he values in good character actors are a sense of humour, a keen eye for the particular physical habits and mannerisms of people, a good ear for the specifics of accent and dialect and, of course, the necessary skills to transmute detailed observation into a sharply defined and singular character.

Casting is done by means of an interview and work-out. In the auditions for the film of *Bleak Moments* and for *Hard Labour* he would interview individual actors and then work with them in small groups on improvised situations. The situations he chose were ones which tended 'to lend themselves to hysteria'. A funeral was a typical situation for these audition improvisations.

I described the man who's died and said to the actors: 'You've got to decide on who your character is, based on someone you know.' I made them spend some time in a corner by themselves, and then they'd come, in character, to this funeral.

The way in which the actors 'played a scene', which was potentially highly fraught and emotional, enabled him to 'sort out those who were going to cod it' from those who understood that 'you didn't have to project grief or woe'.

What was being assessed was the actor's capacity to internalise, and this is still the case in the auditions he runs today. But nowadays he auditions actors for an hour or two at a time and they always work alone with him. The audition takes the form, in a sketchy way, of the first stages of the actual rehearsals. The actor is invited to talk about a specific person he knows and then to work at bringing that person into existence. Leigh insists on a work-out even with actors whose stage work is well known and regardless of their professional reputation or public celebrity.

Quite apart from the most important objective of Leigh's process of auditioning, which is to find good actors with whom he can work, this meticulous and time-consuming procedure serves another purpose. A work-out at the casting stage takes away some of the mystery of the actual working method and there is less likelihood of the actor being overawed or inhibited when he begins to rehearse. For there are, even now, some enormous misconceptions about what working with Leigh involves. 'The myth is that a gang of actors get together with a director and out of the four walls of their ivory tower there comes out of their bowels and out of their souls and their psyche a kind of vision.' The machinery whereby this vision agglomerates is imagined to be a kind of collective soul-baring where the actor, naked, vulnerable and raw probes the forbidden recesses of his secret self to discover the profound mystery of truth. Well, vision and truth there may be, but they're achieved through entirely practical means and in a down-to-earth manner. Leigh would agree with the sign which used to hang in Brecht's room: 'The truth is always concrete.' When the actor is cast any notions of his being about to become involved in a magical/fantastical/psychic experience will have been disposed of. The work is going to be about the experiences and disciplines of acting.

For his own part, the actor agrees to participate in the making of the play or film but, in principle, he doesn't concern himself with what it's going to be about. In the case of stage plays the actor is told that 'Everyone is going to have a good part and no-one's going to sit in the dressing-room all night.' In *Ecstasy*, although there is one character who appears in one short scene and another who appears in two, most of the characters are on stage for almost the whole of the play. The same is true of Leigh's other later stage plays – *Bleak Moments, Babies Grow Old, Abigail's Party and Goose-Pimples*. In addition to the impressive consistency with which Leigh fulfils his commitment to the actors in this regard, the form of the stage plays is partly determined by this promise.

With his films Leigh doesn't make any commitment of this kind. The medium of film allows a greater flexibility in the disposition of a larger number of characters, but there are other reasons to do with film financing. *Grown-Ups*, which is an extremely concentrated look at a period in the lives of six characters – and this respect it's very close in spirit to the form of the stage plays – is the only film where Leigh has had all the actors at his disposal from the first day of rehearsal to the last day of shooting. Although this meant that 'you can do anything you want with any combinations of characters or relationships', it was only possible with a relatively small cast. In order to get round the problem of having only a few characters in a film, he works what he calls a 'pyramid process of getting a cast for a film'. Film budgeting is such that with *x* thousand pounds to spend on actors 'you can either have, as it were, one actor for fifty weeks or fifty actors for one week.' It becomes practical, therefore, to take on two actors, for example, in week one; two more in week two; two more in week three and so on. Working in this way inevitably determines in advance which characters the film is going to centre on.

Actors in stage plays are contracted for the entire rehearsal period. The period of rehearsal prior to the beginning of shooting is budgeted by Leigh within, for example, the BBC's production strictures for eight weeks. The actor's job, for the first period of rehearsal, is 'improvisation and research'.

Because of the work-out at the audition stage, when the actor arrives at his first rehearsal he's already on fairly familiar ground. He will have been asked to make a list of people he knows. 'I say, "Think of everybody you can; make a list of everybody you can possibly think of."' At the time of *Individual Fruit Pies* Leigh qualified this task by asking the actors to select a potential bed-sitter tenant, but now he's much less specific. The only qualifications are that the people on the list have to be the same sex as the actor and that they must be close to the actor's age.[1] Leigh and the actor now sit

1. This apparently uncontroversial statement illustrates the difficulty of making any *general* statements about Leigh's method without suggesting that it's all systematic. There are plenty of times when he's laid down qualifications. Richard Ireson, for example, who came late into the pyramid to play the policeman in *Nuts in May*, was asked to choose a person who could, under certain circumstances, be violent. Eric Allan, a reasonably young man, played an old man in *Too Much of a Good Thing*, because radio doesn't involve worries about actors' appearances. I must emphasise that the working principles are what's being described and that the principle, here, is that Leigh likes to allow himself the greatest possible freedom and creative scope to make his choices. This book, however, only covers his work up to *Home Sweet Home* and he's quite likely to change the way he selects characters in future projects without compromising this principle.

down alone, with no other members of the cast present nor anyone from the production team, and talk through the list of real people in very great detail for as long as it takes. The actor is encouraged to be idiosyncratic and particular in his talk and the conversation is allowed to be 'slow, open-ended, rambling and erratic'. To have, in short, all the characteristics of any interesting chat between relaxed people. The emphasis, from the very first moments, is on the personal tempo of the actor.

It's important for the discussion at this stage to be anecdotal, specific and to get into detail because one's going to want to be all those things later on when we're actually acting. It's important to get into that rhythm.

A great deal of time is spent in this leisurely and discursive business, the primary object of which is to select a person from the list for the actor to turn into a character. It can be especially long for an actor with whom Leigh's never worked before, or with actors with lots of people on their lists. Furthermore, actors are discouraged from glossing details and from censoring themselves – 'Oh, you won't want to hear about this.' 'Yes, I do. Let's enjoy it.'

In this intensely particular period of discussion, while the activity is reviewing the actors' lists, a pattern of principle is being laid down for subsequent work in rehearsal. 'Most actors' says Leigh, 'are conditioned to having to be quick and not thinking in terms of the idiosyncratic, interesting things that life's about.' By releasing actors from the pressure 'to be quick' and from having immediately to deliver the goods, Leigh's work does much more than give them the freedom to sit back and have a natter. It represents a fundamentally different experience of work from that which most actors are used to, and an implicit acknowledgement of the creative possibilities of acting.

Generally speaking, the freedom to create a thoroughly motivated character whose essential individuality can be explored at depth is an enormous and, alas, rare luxury for the actor.

Most acting, most of the time, isn't motivated by anything other than the *actor's* motivation. There isn't any *character* motivation.

More often than not the actor is the last person responsible for this state of affairs.

In the end much of what is motivated by actors in performance arises from the strictures and limitations of the way plays are rehearsed. You don't get a chance to investigate anything but the specific scene and the way that scene is going to be staged. That is still the case and it's all so primitive and elementary.

Whether as actors, directors or as members of audiences we are bound to acknowledge the truth of this observation. Stanislavski may tell us that 'every artistic stage character is a unique, individual creation like everything else in nature'[2] but only a precious few of our actors transcend the individuality of their own mannerisms, habits and other manifestations of personal style to give us characters who appear upon the stage as authentic living people. When such moments occur, the critics usually pounce on them, as they have done in review upon review of Leigh's plays, singling them out for what Antony Curtis has called 'triumphs in the art of acting'.[3]

This enthusiasm for the performances in Leigh's work (which is usually

2. David Magarshack, *Stanislavski on the Art of the Stage*, Hill & Wang, 1961.

3. *Critics' Forum*, BBC Radio 3, 14 March 1981.

accompanied by indifference to its content and about which there will be more to say) is, in its own way, some measure of how far he goes beyond the 'strictures and limitations' of most rehearsal practices into the creative potential of his actors, presenting performances of specific artistry rather than generalised competence.

When Leigh chats to the actor about the people on his list, he is taking the actor on the first steps into the creative process in a way that's saying: Be specific because that's interesting; your observations are worthwhile and will be taken seriously; the work we're doing is going to be rooted in real life; develop your objective eye in your description. The total of all this for the actor is the conviction that 'what he's doing is completely uncompromisable by what anyone else is doing'.

More subtly, a distribution of responsibilities is occurring which can, perhaps, be best illustrated by reference to a workshop Leigh conducts at the Actor's Centre and elsewhere. He asks actors to select a character they have played recently. Each actor is asked a series of questions which he is to answer quietly for himself.

Who were you actually playing? Who were you actually being? Yourself? Or the character? If you were being yourself, why should you be the source of the character? If you were being the character, who is the character? What was the source for your characterisation?

There follows a series of questions about the source of the characterisation? 'Was it from your own head? From the movies? From somebody you know? From somebody else's performance?'

There are questions about the development of the character. 'Did who you were being change from one stage to another?' And some questions about the condition in which the character existed: 'Was he more or less or averagely relaxed?' It's predictable that ninety-five per cent of people say 'averagely so' because the character was pitched any old place. He asks them to change the character's state of relaxation and to explore the consequences of this change. Finally they are asked to:

Think of someone you know who could be the model for this character. Now go into character and use that person, do that person in the character's situation. Now, make that person *be* the character. Now go through the scene in the play, just monitor your way through it.

By the end of this workshop, 'people discover things they never got anywhere near in performance.'

What we have here is not a recital to the actor of the way a part should be played. The direction is not *descriptive*. The actor is turned in upon his own resources and left to come up with the answers. He's asked to define the source of the characterisation – is it general or particular – to explore the condition of the character – where was it pitched? – and finally to discover what would happen to the character when it's based on a specific real-life model. The exploration, discovery and definition is the actor's freedom. The questioning, channelling and focusing of attention is the director's prerogative.

This workshop is too simple an event to serve as an example of Leigh's work with actors in its entirety, but it does illustrate the way in which responsibilities are balanced in the making of his plays and films and how, in particular, the tension between the actor's freedom and the director's control is resolved. The partnership is based on the director's implicit belief in the actor as a creative individual and the actor's trust in the director's ability to set up appropriate rehearsal tasks through which the character and the play may grow. These principles are not articulated at the time, or ever, as far as I know, unless actors are commenting upon the process with hindsight. The actor simply absorbs them through the pores of his skin, allowing them to determine the rhythm and detailed quality of his work.

Talking through the actor's list of real people can take several days and in parallel with the discussion with one actor there are similar discussions with each of the other actors. If all the actors have brought long lists to the rehearsals the number of real people talked about can form a multitude. Leigh keeps very detailed notes during this phase. When all the lists have been talked out he begins to consider ways in which some of the people the actors have discussed might be brought together. This invariably means going back to the actor and getting him to talk about certain people from his list in relation to each other. He might be asked, for example, which of the two men, A and B, is 'more reflective'; or, of the women X, Y and Z, 'compare them in terms of how they would have felt when they lost their virginity'. Such questions invite the actor to probe the people a little more and reveal to Leigh more substance on which to base his eventual decisions.

At this stage the options which are being weighed up, and the choices which are soon to be made as to which of the real people is to be selected for the actor to work on, all happen within the context of the possible relationships which could exist between clusters of characters based on originals whom Leigh finds, for one reason or another, inherently interesting. Sometimes the selection of the person requires an additional kick and the actor is asked to see if he can 'dredge up someone else' because – and this is a confidence rarely shared with the actor – 'it's a blank' even after all the full lists have been considered. Working intuitively, and without reference to plot, story or theme, Leigh simply can't find the way in which characters might interrelate, or why one character should be chosen in preference to another.

Similarly, there can be difficulties in perceiving what qualities certain people possess which makes them sufficiently different from each other for an interesting and varied texture to emerge. Sometimes, too, an interesting person comes off the actor's list and suggests a clear avenue of development which Leigh will deliberately not pursue because it seems too close to something he's already explored in a previous film or play.

It can appear to the actor that the eventual selection of the character is a pretty arbitrary matter, although this is rarely the case.

If you ask an actor what happened, he'll say, 'Well, I talked to Mike for ages and I told him about these people and eventually he picked one. I don't know why he picked that one.'

The actor sees one person from his list being chosen but no particular reason for the selection. It's a point of principle that he will not be told the reason even though the choice may be of a person he knows less well than some of the others or it excludes one 'favourite' person that he might have been looking forward to working on.

While the actor sees one person being selected, Leigh selects (in the case of the stage plays) five or six, possibly from a total number of nearly two hundred. His selection is guided by some notion about the possibilities of their interaction. The notion can come from anywhere. If he's spent more than a week talking about scores of people, the material for a play can sometimes be suggested by the details of 'lives, cultures and biographies' unearthed during the conversations, but on other occasions people are selected solely on the basis of their own inherent interest and in the expectation that something interesting will happen when they all get brought together as characters. In these instances, the discussions will have yielded nothing substantial by way of suggestions for the action of a play. There are times, too, when with one person hardening in his mind Leigh will go back to the other actors to explore further some of the people on their lists in the context of the one decision he's already made.

While this is certainly an unconventional way of taking the first steps into the creation of a play it would be, as Clive Hodgson says, a mistake to see it as 'a deviation from the norm of creative activity'. Hodgson's observations on Leigh's way of working are practical and sensible:

> Essentially the creation of a Mike Leigh play is not really different from that of any other play, in that ideas are formulated, possibilities are explored, some possibilities are disregarded, others are developed and the various elements are brought together to create a finished dramatic piece. And the only substantial difference is that actors are involved from the very beginning in a Mike Leigh play whereas in most plays they're brought in half-way through that process.[4]

These early rehearsals represent, in conventional terms, the stage at which the writer sifts and arranges his ideas, makes character sketches and begins in other ways to define his material.

Clive Hodgson's point will stand a bit more emphasis because it's so central to a full understanding of Leigh's method. In his review of *Goose-Pimples*, B.A. Young spoke of the play in terms of 'plays that are devised by a director and have the details filled in at rehearsal by the company'.[5] What this suggests is that the director somehow imagines a collection of characters, a situation, a plot and a resolution and that the actors, through improvisation, provide the dialogue and the blocking. The idea that Leigh's plays and films are assembled in this manner is very wide of the mark but it's been put forward so often that it persists in many people's minds as being true.

Let's look for a moment at a play (or a film) as working on three broad levels: its action or narrative – ie., what happens between the characters – what they do and what they say; its themes and ideas – what the play finds to say about or through the human incidents it shows; its style, although with Leigh's work I'd prefer, for now, to use the word texture.

Now Young suggests that the action of *Goose-Pimples*, and by implication of all Leigh's plays and films, is predetermined. The fact is that such a thing is completely impossible because action is what characters do and when Leigh begins work he doesn't even know who the characters are. In certain instances he has known more about the general outline of a project than others, but that's not the same thing as knowing what the action will be.

When he began work on *Nuts in May*, for example, he really knew quite a lot about it.[6] Its main characters, Keith and Candice Marie Pratt, had been created originally in

4. *Kaleidoscope*, BBC Radio 4, 6 March 1981.

5. *Financial Times*, 4 March 1981.

6. It wasn't called *Nuts in May* until it was finished; its working title was 'The Plastic Tadpole'. It's a BBC requirement that all projects must have titles. Other working titles for BBC projects conjure up an unlikely menagerie. *Hard Labour* was 'The Electric Weasel'; *The Permissive Society* was 'The Clockwork Chipmunk'; *Knock for Knock*, 'The Elastic Peanut'; *The Kiss of Death*, 'The Concrete Mongrel'; *Who's Who*, 'The Porcelain Pig'; *Too Much of a Good Thing*, 'The Chocolate Chicken'; *Grown-Ups*, 'The Iron Frog'; and *Home Sweet Home*, 'The Wooden Egg'. There's more to this than mere whimsy. The plays and films aren't given titles until he can be sure that the title will be right. The absurdity of the working title reinforces the point that he doesn't know the content when he starts work and confers the freedom for work to be about anything.

a stage play, *Wholesome Glory,* so he knew a great deal about them. The film's producer, David Rose, had suggested Dorset as a location for the shooting and Leigh had agreed that it was to be about the Pratts on holiday and that it would contrast their humourless, busybodying zeal with the more relaxed and casual enjoyment of other holiday-makers.

None of these ideas, however, had found a form other than in the previous existence of Keith and Candice Marie. When the company got together to start rehearsing for *Nuts in May* they created many new characters, new situations and, ultimately, new action out of which the material of the film was made. While what they did fell in with the general contours of the agreed outline, at no time was what specifically occurs in the film predictable.

Hard Labour provides an even sharper example. It was Leigh's first film for the BBC and the fact that it was made at all is principally due to the efforts of its producer, Tony Garnett, to whom Leigh acknowledges an enormous debt: 'he really put his head on the chopper'. It was clear that there would have to be some specific commitment as to the theme and content of the film since the BBC would not authorise and finance the work of a young, unconventional and still relatively unknown director, no matter how hard Garnett worked on his behalf.

Basing his ideas for the film on his own experiences of growing up and living in Salford, Leigh proposed that *Hard Labour* should be about Mrs Thornley and her working-class family, a middle-class family and an immigrant family. By fusing his own autobiographical concerns with other ideas which had been amplified in his discussions with Garnett, Leigh began work with a substantial premise for the film and a cast which reflected all these ideas directly:

There were two middle-aged couples. There was a complete family for the Thornleys. There was an Indian family.

But as soon as rehearsals started, the literal origins of *Hard Labour* 'all got lost'.

As I began to get into it and as the actual world we were creating took on its reality, I began to sort out what it was actually about.

The preconceptions which he'd taken into rehearsal gave way to other ideas which became the content of the film. Instead of a semi-autobiographical film comparing three sets of family life, *Hard Labour* is a remorseless and compassionate investigation of the life of one woman in the context of her own family, the leisured existence of the woman for whom she cleans and an entire urban world of class, religion, culture and money going on around her. It's a study of, among other things, personal alienation.

The examples of *Nuts in May* and *Hard Labour* illustrate not only how misleading and wrong is the suggestion that the action of Leigh's works is decided in advance. They also demonstrate that themes and ideas for a film or play exist before narrative and action, but that they, too, are susceptible to re-investigation and fresh definition in the actual work of rehearsal. This is hardly a startling and original observation but I am at pains to point out that although Leigh works differently from most dramatists, his process is essentially the same as any artist's.

The themes and ideas for work can be at various stages of development when Leigh begins rehearsing. When he started *Goose-Pimples* he knew that he wanted to do a play –

which looked at, in a fairly hard and slightly grotesque and comic way, the 1981 world of the crumbling pound and the way in which cars and petrol and wealth and jobs and all those things are hysterically clung to.[7]

The first glimmerings of a way in which these ideas could be broached didn't occur until in the discussion of the people on her list Marion Bailey talked about three women who had had dealings with Arabs. When he did *Who's Who* he knew that it would involve a contrast in class attitudes and relationships because the producer, Margaret Matheson, had suggested that he might look at some upper-class characters for a change. When he began *Grown-Ups* he 'didn't know what it was going to be about'. In terms of themes and ideas he says that it doesn't really matter '*whether* an idea exists but *when* the idea exists'.

In fact, some ideas exist all the time for, again in common with all artists, there are consistent areas of concern about life which he wishes to explore, and these tend to coalesce in his work around a figure or figures who are somehow alienated from themselves or from society and around the fact of social class.

I do not see class as a 'structure', nor even as a 'category' but, as something which in fact happens . . . in human relationships.[8]

The words are E. P. Thompson's but they could as well be Leigh's own. Social class is more than a theme or an idea in Leigh's work, it's its fundamental reality, the principal web in its fabric. Class is the implicit condition of the character's lives, informing and shaping their culture, language, behaviour, attitudes, relationships and sense of self. The fact of social class expressed in human relationships is a broad background of concern against which Leigh balances and measures the people he selects from the actors' lists.

I said at the beginning of this discussion that I preferred the word texture to style as a way of defining the third level of Leigh's plays and films. This isn't an unnecessary semantic quibble, but an attempt to be accurate, because he sometimes knows the feel of a play before the themes have become clear and the characters have formed. Before he went into rehearsal for *Abigail's Party* he knew that he wanted it to be 'a boulevard play on the surface'. It was to have the 'atmosphere and gloss, the pace and brittle surface' of a sleek bourgeois comedy. *Ecstasy,* his next play at Hampstead, was to be a self-consciously different. It was to be about working-class life, 'drab and downbeat' in atmosphere. *Goose-Pimples,* which followed *Ecstasy,* was to be different again, 'a kind of anti-farce'.

There can be many impulses towards a play in Leigh's mind when he begins his discussions with the actors but there is never a detailed sense of narrative and action. In any case, at this stage, narrative and action are the last things he's thinking about. When the time arrives for these elements to be considered, they form only the tip of an enormous iceberg, the main substance of which has been created during the process of rehearsal.

Once he has selected one person for each actor to work on Leigh's next step is to set about bringing that person to life through a process which starts as a detailed imitation of the original and then develops into the formation of a new character. The work continues with each actor on his own.

All the individual work of characterisation is bound by a strict code of secrecy. For a long time Leigh used to hang one of Fougasse's famous World War II posters,

7. *Start the Week,* BBC Radio 4, 27 April 1981.

8. E. P. Thompson, *The Making of the English Working Class,* Gollancz, 1963.

'CARELESS TALK COSTS LIVES', in the rehearsal room. The slogan is literally true. The purpose of these private, solo rehearsals is for the actor to create a character with an entirely individual and particular identity. If the actors were to talk to each other about their characters it's easy to imagine how they might begin to try to fit them together, making, perhaps unconsciously, compromises and accommodations in their own impulses. Equally damagingly they might begin to surmise about the nature of the finished piece and become self-conscious about the narrative nature of subsequent improvisations.

The code of secrecy is much more than a rule which exists for its own sake. It's the practical expression of one of the fundamentals of Leigh's work as a dramatist. The writer who sits at home shaping his characters in his mind and on paper doesn't have the problem of the characters leaking into each other, if he's any good, so there's never any danger of them losing their integrity as characters. They exist, as it were, in separate mental compartments, so they don't get in the way of each other's development. For Leigh, who doesn't work in the study but on the rehearsal room floor, the convention of secrecy is his way of maintaining the rights, prerogatives and freedoms of the writer.

More than this, the independent and uncompromised development of completely particular characters is essential to the exploration and statement of the central concerns of his work. If the plays and films are to seem *real* – and by common consent this is exactly what they do seem – then the characters must grow in a way which simulates reality in the most precise way possible, given the basic conditions of rehearsal rooms and so on. For the finished work to offer a convincing representation of reality, the action and behaviour of the characters must correspond to the action and behaviour of people in real life. The actor's work, therefore, must be to get the reality of his character right before he has to concern himself with what any other actor is up to and before he has to consider what the play or film is about. As Leigh says,

> With this kind of work one character can't afford to know more about another character than he or she would know about any stranger, otherwise the improvisation would be bullshit.[9]

So it is the creation of the character's particular identity which is the content of the next stage of rehearsal, and it is the identity of the actual, original person suggested from the actor's list which is worked on first.

To begin with, the work continues through discussion, but now what is talked about is the life of the particular person in great detail. A specific biography is created out of the known facts of the life of the original model. The discussions will range over both 'the material' and 'the emotional' foundations of the life. For example:

> Who is he? When was he born? Where was he born? Who were his parents? What was his education? What was his socio-economic background? What were his cultural influences? Who were his friends, if he had any? What's his sexual drive? Then – how does he walk? How does he talk? What were his first experiences of one kind and another?

This process is less straightforward than it might at first seem for the amount of information each actor knows about the original can vary, as, indeed, can his attitude

9. Gordon Burn, 'Mike Leigh's Theatre of Embarrassment', Sunday Times Magazine, 10 May 1981.

to what he knows.

It's possible that the actor can be 'lumbered' by Leigh having selected an original about whom the actor, after all, knows very little: someone, perhaps, whom the actor has met only a few times or whom he hasn't seen for years. In this situation, sometimes it's useful for the actor to re-establish contact with the person and sometimes it's not. It's the actor's conception of the original which is important. For some actors a study of the original can be their equivalent of what other artists do, that is, it can be an investigation of an aspect of reality and the drawing together of a number of specific observations for the purposes of creative work. For other actors it's unnecessary because –

We're not doing a photographic portrait of the actual person. The person is just a jumping off point.

So 'what we don't know, we'll make up.' Thus to the few known and verifiable facts of this person's life Leigh adds fictional details, carefully assembled to coincide with and be commensurate with the known information. This kind of approach establishes for the actor the idea that it is the fiction of the play which, at the end of the day, is going to be the most important thing and that the original facts aren't holy.

There's no hard and fast rule as to which of these lines Leigh takes in the creation of a detailed biography. Decisions will be influenced by the attitude of the actor to the amount of information he knows and the kind of person being used as the original source for the character. If, for example, the original's life has taken him into a world about which the actor knows absolutely nothing then, providing that some knowledge of that world is essential to getting the acting going, first hand observation will be both helpful and necessary. If the original's life is a more familiar one – say, university, teacher training and a subsequent teaching job; a pattern which the actor might know a bit about – then it's a simple matter to make up a biography without compromising the truthfulness of the work.

There are occasions, too, when the actor knows so much about his original that the biography accumulates in great factual detail very easily. Too great a respect for the facts can inhibit the actor by cramping the flexibility of his work. If he's allowed to cherish the incontrovertability of the facts the actor may resist moves to adapt to the demands of the fiction because his original 'wouldn't do that'. The biography of this actor's original needs to be created with due regard for the flexibility necessary to render it, eventually, into a character and fiction. Finally, there are sometimes actors who aren't interested in the factual basis of their original's biography and who need to be restrained from work which is 'artificial and decorative'.

The principle which is central to this phase of rehearsal and common to all the work, regardless of the variables, is that a character is being created 'from scratch with constant reference to the source', and that whatever negotiations take place with individual actors, each character will have the roots of its being in real life. Leigh refers to the way in which he brings a unity to these varying attitudes to the creation of biographies as 'that aspect of what I do which is simply good directing: how to handle the actors'. But there's more to it than an exercise in tactful human relations. For the actors are, without any working contact with each other, being brought into a common way of working and a community of style. In practical terms this means that when the actors begin to encounter each other in character a little later on, they will behave and exist in the same dimension as each other, no matter how personal, individual and idiosyncratic that behaviour may be. There will undoubtedly be plenty of times in the subsequent rehearsals when the play is finding its identity that the characters are out of stylistic alignment, but in the early stages each character begins from the same bedrock. On an entirely functional level, the creation of a detailed biography serves to bring the original out of the crowded ranks of the host of people who've been discussed and into the closely observed foreground.

By the end of this phase both Leigh and the actor know all about the life of the actual person on whom the characterisation is to be based. Now the acting can start.

There are two distinct phases in the rehearsal of Leigh's plays and films: 'pre-rehearsal' and 'structuring'.

Pre-rehearsal

Pre-rehearsal is the period in which the actors talk through their lists, originals are selected, characters are created, brought to life and changed, extended and modified; it's when the characters meet each other and when the substance of their lives together is created through extensive improvisation and research.

Structuring

Structuring is the period when the play is made up and rehearsed or when sequences of action are polished prior to their being filmed.

Pre-rehearsal is essentially the equivalent of the writer's note-making stage, in which possibilities for the play are explored. But while the parallel with the solitary writer is useful as a means of identifying the purpose of pre-rehearsal, it cannot reflect its complexity. It is here that the relationship between Leigh's authorship of the plays and his work as a director is at its most dense, because the substance of pre-rehearsal occurs through three-dimensional acting in which a number of things are happening simultaneously. There are two basic areas of work in pre-rehearsal: 'narrative' and 'behaviour'.

Narrative work

This means improvisation and discussion which creates the content of the characters; it covers their biographies and the stories of what happens to them together, their conflicts and relationships. It covers the actual events of their lives, in the present, in the past and in memory.

Behaviour work

Behaviour embraces their ideas, their culture, their consciousness and their physical characteristics: how they walk and talk; their bearing and posture, manner and mannerisms and the interrelationship between all these things.

It is quite apparent that these elements overlap with each other constantly, but for the sake of clarity they may be looked at separately, and it's the part of the work which has to do with narrative that I'll take first. The creation of the biography of the person who is to be the source for the character is part of the narrative thrust of the rehearsals. When the actor gets to his feet for the first time, it's the narrative element which continues to be developed.

The acting begins by 'finding for each character – at first the actual original – an extant current time present in which to place him'. Chronological time is the mesh which holds the narrative improvisations together. There is no darting about among the details of the original's past to find out what he did here, how he felt there. The improvisations begin at a certain point and progress from there in an orderly and systematic sequence. The same discipline governs the later narrative improvisations when the characters are brought together.

The moment of time present in which the original is placed is informed by all the discussion of the person's biography which has gone before. Leigh gives an example of the way in which the acting might now be set up:

'Let's decide that of the various times in this guy's life that we've talked about, let's say that we're actually looking at 1959' – or 1966 or whenever – 'and it was then that you said he was at college and was going out with this girl. Now let's decide that he's been going out with her for two years.' You can then fill in that retrospectively, and say, 'Right, if it's Friday, he saw her on Wednesday; what happened on that occasion?' And you might take an hour to discuss what happened and then you've established yet something else. Then you might ask, 'When did he last see his mother?' 'That was two weeks ago.' Then, 'What's his financial situation at the moment?' etc . . .

All these establishing circumstances are highly specific, particular and related to a precise instant in time. 'They make it possible for both of you to believe in this person,' and thus it becomes possible to say,

'Right. It is that evening. He's by himself and he's in that room. Go into character and see what happens.'

The actor has probably been coming to rehearsals for over a fortnight and this is the first time he's been asked to do any acting. This deceleration of their usual work rate is a further reinforcement, if one is needed, of Leigh's principle of liberating actors from the need to be instantly entertaining. His purpose is 'to get them away from the idea of having to be interesting, illuminating, funny or sad, but having to be real.'

This principle is carried right into the first moments of acting when the actor is told,

'Don't make anything happen for effect. Don't concern yourself with putting it across to me. In fact, I will leave you alone for a few minutes.'

As soon as the actor takes on the role of the original source (and in their own individual rehearsals the other members of the cast are doing the same) the resources of the production are brought in to support him in the creation of a believable time-present reality. Leigh uses a number of flexible screens which can be arranged to simulate the rooms in which the characters live. These 'rooms' will be of the appropriate dimensions to the characters' circumstances and will be furnished with the appropriate fittings. Similarly, the right clothes are used.

From now on the character is explored in a series of improvisations which unfold chronologically. To develop the example given above, if the character's acted life begins on a Friday evening in 1959, the next improvisation will probably be on the following Saturday morning, and the next, the Saturday afternoon and so on, and thus will continue to cover a few days, a week, a month or even years in the character's life.

In terms of narrative, each step along the line of chronology accumulates the character's actual experience on a number of levels: what he did, how he felt; what he thought and so on. In parallel with this, the actor is learning how to play the character and becoming confident and fluent in his portrayal. He's also learning how to control the character, for after each improvisation Leigh asks him to come out of character and to analyse what happened.

There are two strands to this analysis. The first is concerned with what happened to the character, why he behaved as he did; whether anything 'new' or 'uncharacteristic' occurred in his action, thinking or feeling? Out of this analysis both Leigh and the actor develop a fuller understanding of the character and hints and suggestions for further exploration. To use Stanislavski's terminology for a moment, each improvisation creates a new set of 'given circumstances' for the next. If, for example, while making a cup of coffee in his 'room' the character suddenly becomes angry because he knocked over the milk, or couldn't find a cup, that burst of short-temperedness becomes something to investigate, and modifies the premises on which the next improvisation in the sequence will be based.

As far as the actor is concerned, how the character is played opens up a different path of analysis. The actor may be having trouble engaging with the character because of tentativeness, or misapplication of energy. Or he may simply be getting things wrong for himself by failing to identify sufficiently precisely the original's posture, or movement quality. He might be anxious that the character is not apparently 'doing enough', a common worry among actors who are conditioned to the instant business of most conventional rehearsal procedures.

The experience of the actor and the experience of the character are obviously interrelated, but they are nevertheless different and this is one of the reasons why Leigh looks for objectivity in his actors and why he reinforces it by insisting that both he and the actor refer to the character in the third person.

An integral part of developing the reality of the character is for the actor to be able 'to do what the character does' and if this means making forays beyond the walls of the rehearsal room to do some shopping for example or to take a walk in the park, then, when he is sufficiently fluent and confident in his work, this is what the actor in character, will do. There is a notion that Leigh makes his actors go shopping in character as some kind of test, but it's not a test at all, merely a logical extension of the character's activity. There is no compulsion to it.

When the actors have their characters on firm foundations they are brought together in the next phase of pre-rehearsal. It isn't always easy to set up a common basis of experience as the premise for the next set of improvisations. Because the actors have been working alone in rehearsals where the principal emphasis has been on the individuality of their characters, adjustments are usually necessary to bring everyone to the same point of time and circumstances so that a fresh set of chronologically governed improvisations may be launched.

In nearly all Leigh's plays and films the narrative eventually focuses on a densely linked cluster of interrelationships. All these relationshps have to be brought into being by one means or another and the first step is to realign the characters' sense of time so that, for example, a character whose solitary life was set in 1980 does not find himself with another character who firmly believes that he exists in 1983. Sometimes changes not only of time, but also of culture have to be accommodated.

All the improvisation work I've described so far has been what Leigh calls 'figurative'. That is, the improvisations are taken to be real events in real time occurring three-dimensionally so that an outsider viewing them could, *mutatis mutandis,* believe them actually to be taking place. Thus, the example, in which the character knocked over the milk, is a figurative improvisation.

In the business of realigning the characters, however, figurative improvisation is not always necesssary because the realignments may be accomplished by other means. 'There are,' says Leigh, 'two classic ways of getting a relationship going.' The first is for the characters to meet in figurative improvisation; the other is for the actors to sit down and invent a fresh set of joint biographies.

There's a drawback to the characters' meeting each other in improvisation and that is that the actors know what they're in the improvisation for so the outcome of the improvisation becomes predictable. Character meetings, therefore, tend to be functionally useful in that they provide a living memory for the characters, but in terms of their dramatic potential they're usually 'memorably banal'. Sylvia and Peter from *Bleak Moments* met on a train. Tony and Angela from *Abigail's Party* met as patient and nurse in hospital and Beverly and Laurence met in Laurence's office when she came to temp there. None of these encounters was, in itself, interesting, and thus were never mentioned in the plays or films.

When the actors create a joint biography for their characters the problem is that none of the details of their shared past become real to them until the characters have experience of each other in figurative improvisation. There are no foundations in the relationship other than Leigh's simply bringing it into existence – 'These two people are mother and daughter' he will tell the actors. Nevertheless, it's often necessary to create relationships in this way, because you can't have actors pretending to be babies.' Thus, usually it's the family histories of blood relations which are created by the actors making up the details, while characters who are married have generally been through the whole experience of their relationship in figurative improvisation.

This business of realignment can be a tricky stage in pre-rehearsal, but the fact that it's negotiated successfully is a testament to the compositional freedom of the method. It's a testament, too, to another important element in Leigh's work which should not be overlooked: its spirit of creative fun. In describing the salient features of this intense, disciplined and scrupulously professional rehearsal process I don't mean to convey the sense that it's also po-faced, self-serious and bit precious. There's a lot of laughter and enjoyment in these reheasals, but it's not the laughter of those who make jokes to evade serious work. 'Nobody who fails to get fun out of his activities can expect them to be fun for anybody else,' wrote Brecht.[10] It's in harmony with this sentiment that Leigh's rehearsals are conducted.

Once the characters are working together in figurative improvisations the narrative content becomes more dense and the ramifications of the relationships multiply. Each single improvisation may yield dozens of possibilities for further investigation, and sequences of improvisations continue to accumulate the characters' experience, intensify their conflicts and deepen the collective reality.

What happens moment to moment depends, as it does in all this work, on the specific elements of the particular play and it's no more possible to generalise about the content of this phase of rehearsal than it is with any other. The principle, however, is constant. Each improvisation is a real event in the characters' lives, and as such everything is significant for the characters and for the developing play.

To make this clear I want to use the extended and fictitious example of an

10. John Willett, *Brecht on Theatre,* Hill & Wang/Eyre Methuen, 1964.

improvisation in which three characters, Alan, Bob and Chris, sit and drink tea with each other and talk about sport (or whatever). It's a dense event because beneath the surface is an entire sub-textual world of the people's aspirations, fantasies, frustrations, past experiences, desires, needs and preoccupations. Remembering that this is only a simple example, we might say that within the context of the conversation Alan is trying to present himself in a positive way in order to be liked by Bob. Bob wants to impress Chris in order that Chris will be in awe of him and Chris wants them both to go away because Diane is arriving in a minute and if the others are there, there'll be a row. Adding to this the conditions that Alan is dog-tired because he's been up all night, that Bob actually knows nothing about football and is trying to change the subject and that Chris would rather die than give offence to anyone, it should be clear that the situation can be one of some complexity. This example only offers two premises for each character. In Leigh's rehearsals the characters have been formed independently over some weeks of intensive work and come to these situations literally packed with premises. The situation's complexity is proportionately increased.

But it is only acting. The example isn't of three people actually sitting talking about football but of three actors playing these people within a carefully contrived fiction. The difference from real life is that you can stop it and either tinker about with the characters' internal conditions or alter them radically so long as any changes allow the actor still to make sense of the character. Thus it's possible to analyse with each of the actors what happened to his character in the improvisation.

The actor playing Alan might have found that this tiredness was making the character irritable. The director might see in Alan's irritability the possibility of a sharp conflict. With a suggestion that as the conversation goes on Alan might become even more tired, he's allowed to continue much as before, along the same principal line of motivation. Bob, the actor discovers, is not getting very far in impressing Chris. There could be much discussion of what Bob will do in this situation, but for the sake of this example, let's say the director and the actor agree that Bob's motivation is such that his failure to get through to Chris would result in Bob's taking a dislike to him. Chris, the actor says, is almost desperate. He has to get rid of them before Diane arrives but can't find a tactful way of asking them to leave. His desperation is so great that some kind of emotional crisis seems imminent. The director might see here a possibility that Chris is going to behave in a way no one expects. The actor might be reminded that the event Chris is dreading, the arrival of Diane, is only a few minutes away and then the actors are brought back together again, get into character and continue to play the situation from the point at which they left off. Chris does explode and try to kick them out. Alan is so irritated by Chris's behaviour that he loses his temper and Bob, because he's never going to let Chris push him around anyway, makes a stand and tries to humiliate Chris in front of Alan. The action is stopped again. The actors come out of character, analyse what's happened, and with more adjustments of the premises, the improvisation is picked up again from where it left off.

This is, I confess, an over-simplified example but it illustrates a number of points, I think, about Leigh's method.

1 All action is the result of the characters' motivations. In order to create action, therefore, work has to be done at the level of motivation and not of action. This is the difference between saying to the actors 'Have a row!' and investigating the circumstances of potential conflicts. The former is closed-ended and descriptive, the latter open-ended and free.

2 In order for motivation to exist, the characters' individual and collective reality must be credible. Changes in motivation, therefore, if they are to occur must always make sense within the bounds of the reality. The actor playing Chris, therefore, can't simply be told 'assert yourself' or 'be more definite' since that sudden change violates both the condition of Chris and the others' belief in him.

3 Each improvisation, as a real event for the characters, grows organically out of what has gone before. There can be no introduction of sudden, arbitrary factors for the sake of effect. In the example given, there would be no suggestion to the actor playing Alan that he should suddenly drop his intention of impressing Bob and turn his attention instead to Chris. If, however, the actor said that Alan, in spite of tiredness was finding something in Chris which he liked and had never seen before, then the director might suggest that he pursue the business of finding Chris likeable.

4 The actors must not know the motivations of each others' characters. This would really mess things up, because if the actors knew what was happening in the sub-textual world of each others' characters the focus of the improvisations would change completely and the result would be a kind of theatre game rather than improvisation for a play. And anyway, it would be another violation of the reality, because the characters would suddenly be privy to each others deepest secrets, dreams and yearnings in a way that people rarely are in life. Of course the *characters'* understanding some of each others' motivations is an entirely different thing. If Bob sees damned well that Alan's trying to impress him, that creates another level of reality for the character.

5 The improvisations are discussed always in terms of real events and never as 'scenes'. The pre-rehearsals are not form-orientated, they are an investigation of content.

There are a couple of other things to mention about the way of working illustrated in this example. First, the event which occurred in the improvisation might never find its way into the finished play at all. Pre-rehearsal is not the hunt for action and text but the investigation of motivation and sub-text, so while the audience might never see the row between Alan, Bob and Chris, it will nevertheless exist implicitly in the play as part of their experience informing that portion of their lives which the audience will see.

Next, the example, of necessity simplified, doesn't suggest specifically enough the backgrounds of the three characters. For, in Leigh's work, it wouldn't be only the raw human situation which informed this improvisation but the whole material and emotional substructure of the characters' world and the way in which their cultural experience, and their class background, shapes the way in which they relate to each other.

Alan, perhaps, has a working-class background, has been to a lot of soccer matches, knows the teams, the players and strategies. Bob, a middle-class character, could be a rugger man and Chris, lower middle-class, enjoys football but expresses his interest in the received language of the sporting columns of the *Guardian* and the *Sunday Times*. Similarly, Chris's being unable to get Alan and Bob to leave need not be the product of timidity but of the taboos in his background against appearing rude.

To the dynamics of the basic human situation is added the complication of language and culture and another layer of tension. While for the actors the life and behaviour of their characters are entirely real, for the director/dramatist the improvisation is working not only as an encounter with its own resonances between three people but, in an embryonic way as an image of a stratified society occurring in a three-dimensional and concrete form.

A further point to consider is the nature of the experience of acting. Not only does each moment of this improvisation increase the store of the character's experience for the actor, it also demands that the actor, in character, responds to events with the spontaneity of real life. Improvisation, by definition, always implies spontaneity and, for its exercise value, is often used in schools and colleges to provide the experience of spontaneity. But we're talking here about a quality which goes beyond a useful exercise.

A common feature of much improvisation which occurs at a shallow level is 'scriptwriting', where the actor will phrase what he says in a certain way for what he judges to be its effectiveness rather than for its truthfulness, or where he will self-consciously contrive action because he thinks it will look good. Self-conscious scriptwriting is always a tell-tale sign of the level at which an improvisation is pitched, for it indicates that the actor's concentration is usually on the spontaneous projection of himself as a witty, quick-thinking performer rather than on any task which might be embodied in the improvisation.

Because the actors in Leigh's rehearsals are working out of the rich and complex experience of their characters – and it's getting richer and more complex by the minute – their spontaneity manifests itself though the way in which their characters are engaged in each instant of their lives. They simply do not know what's going to happen next. It requires off the moment acting of a very high degree of skill, but the manner is so well learned that by the time the form of the work is fixed and when the actors, therefore, do know what's going to happen next, the spontaneous behaviour of the character can still be played.

The last point I want to make from this example is about the whole art of working in this way. The skill lies in being able to judge, often intuitively, which possibilities for investigation and development to take up and which to leave alone. For not all possibilities are always equally rewarding and there are frequently blind alleys where an area of improvisation will have to be wiped.

I often set things up and pursue things, and although it's generally counter-productive to say 'That didn't go anywhere,' sometimes it doesn't go anywhere, so you just let it go.

During the shooting of *Grown-Ups,* with half the film in the can, Leigh sent the crew away for a long holiday weekend while he worked with the six actors to create the event which would succeed in galvanising the whole thing together by involving all the characters in the same traumatic experience.

Set in Canterbury, *Grown-Ups* concerns two families living uneasily next door to each other. Ralph and Christine Butcher are teachers; Mandy and Dick, their neighbours and Ralph's ex-pupils, work, respectively, in a café and in a hospital kitchen. Mandy and Dick and their friend Sharon, a taciturn pessimist from the British Homes Stores sweet counter, are having trouble with Mandy's sister Gloria, played by Brenda Blethyn, who keeps coming round. Her constant invasion of their privacy is putting a strain on Dick and Mandy's marriage.

All these circumstances had been explored in the half of the film which had already been shot. With the crew away the improvisations continued until Gloria came round one time too many and Dick and Mandy forcibly threw her out of their house. It was in Leigh's mind that when Gloria was thrown out she would not go home, since home had already been well established as a place where she found no comfort; she would, he thought, be more likely to run to the Butchers' next door, thus bringing the two households together. Gloria ran home.

It was only in the discussion after the improvisation that Brenda Blethyn said that, actually, she had made a mistake. Gloria would have gone next door to the Butchers. The improvisation in which she ran home was wiped; the running next door improvisation was set up and the repercussions of that event subsequently investigated, providing the narrative material for the climax of the film.

Narrative content may also be explored through a variety of means which are more abstract than the figurative improvisations, rooted as real events in real time. Leigh describes these means as 'schematic'. He will use schematic methods for a variety of reasons and in many different ways. Once again, there is no 'rule' governing their use, simply a response to the actual circumstances of rehearsals at any given moment. Similarly, there is no fixed set of exercises he employs. Depending upon the nature of the play, the propensities of the actor or the condition of the reality which is being created, he makes up exercises to suit what he wants to accomplish.

It might have become apparent already that figurative improvisations can consume a great deal of time. There is, furthermore, a danger that an actor working solely in figurative improvisation might fall into the trap of believing that his character's life is somehow 'sacrosanct and real'. Schematic improvisations can be used to cut corners and also, simultaneously if need be, to dislodge the actor's sense of temporal reality by reminding him that what he is doing, after all, is participating in the creation of a fiction.

In these circumstances, Leigh might say to a group of actors whose characters are going to spend the day together, that the day will be speeded up and he will call out the passage of time with, perhaps, two minutes representing an hour, while the actors 'monitor in their heads' what's going on. While the day does not accumulate the minute details of the figurative work there remains 'the sense of the experience having happened in real life'.

When they monitor an experience the actors do not go fully into character. They simply filter what is happening through the consciousness of the character, absorbing experience as part of the whole background. Monitoring is a way of travelling light with the character and gathering material to feed into the characterisation. By assuming the consciousness of the character while doing things in his own everyday life, the actor can fill in the character's responses to going shopping in a busy store, for example, or waiting for a bus or eavesdropping a conversation in a queue.

Where actors are improvising marriages and friendships over a long period of time there is the possibility that, as the belief in the relationship deepens, it might become cosy. Schematic work can be undertaken to inject more potentially dramatic material into what might become a warm, untroubled domestic arrangement. In such a case, Leigh might set up the following exercise for the actor and actress playing, say, husband and wife. Working separately from the husband, and out of character at first, in order that the principle of the exercise may become clear to her, the actress playing the wife is asked to move furniture about the room, precisely according to Leigh's instructions, and not to say anything by way of question and complaint while she is doing so. Gradually the instructions become brusque, hard and eventually aggressive and rude. Once the actress has grasped the principle of the activity – that she is being progressively harrassed, the first part of the exercise comes to an end.

Now she is asked to lead the exercise, this time in character, with her husband, also in character, on the receiving end of the orders and bound by the same rule of silent obedience. If the immediate purpose of this exercise is to unsettle domestic cosiness, then it might either reveal tensions and hidden conflicts within the relationship which were already there, or it might actually add an entirely new dimension. As a development of the exercise the husband might be told 'Now answer her back', and that would open up further possibilities.

The results of this kind of schematic work aren't necessarily instant. There might not be any immediate and sudden change in the quality of the figurative improvisations between these characters because new experience has to be bedded in, but another ingredient will have been added to mature or to be coaxed out by further investigation.

There's a very important principle lurking here. The actors are not being asked merely to *do* what their characters would do in any particular situation, but *to find the way* in which their characters would do things which might, at first, appear to run counter to the character, and then to absorb the new material into the character's nature. It's clear that when this work is successful it contributes to dense and multi-layered characterisations as well as extending the dramatic range of a relationship. Implicit in this principle is the idea that the character will not just happen by itself. It has to be made to happen. The material of the character is plastic and mutable. Once again, though, any changes in the way in which the character is wrought are not arbitrarily imposed on the actor. They're dovetailed into all his previous experience of the character so that the character grows and is formed by a constant process of extension rather than by a series of abrupt U-turns or juddering stops and starts.

An exercise Leigh uses quite frequently either to save time or to 'investigate things which would otherwise be uninvestigable', such as the characters' sexual relationships, is the playing of a situation through the hands only, in a non-figurative way. The conventions of this exercise, which originates from Lee Strasberg's days at the New York Actors' Studio and which Leigh learned from James Roose-Evans at RADA, are that the actors kneel with their hands in front of them facing each other on the floor, and without setting out consciously to make the hands 'do anything' they allow the energy of the group to take over and see what the hands will do. The actors are not to look at or talk to each other. Leigh's adaptation of this exercise is that the actors do it in character and that interpreted retrospectively, it may stand as both a representation and an investigation of an event in real life.

Thus, a sexual relationship between two characters often cannot, for obvious reasons, be comprehensively investigated through figurative means. But the hand exercise can investigate the reality of the sexual content of the relationship in an entirely abstracted way. There's no clumsy semi-pornographic puppet show with the hands. The encounter is completely abstracted, and liberated from coyness by the actors' immersion in the real lives and experiences of their characters. Once the exercise has run its course, discussion with the actors out of character will probe what was expressed through the abstraction. 'How long could that be taken to represent? What does it suggest happened?' and so on. The answers to these questions are embodied in the characters' experiences of each other and subsequently inform the later figurative work. The essence of the use of this exercise is that it is a means of investigating moment to moment experiences which are beyond the practical scope of figurative improvisations; it can come to represent a four hour car journey, for example, or an evening in the cinema.

A further area of schematic work on narrative is included in what Leigh calls 'Rituals and Simulations'. In *Bleak Moments,* the central character, Sylvia, has a boring office job. A major part of the characters' experience is her sense of isolation, intensified by there being no fulfilling relationships in her life and no meaning in her work. The dullness of the office routine, however, is a function of real time, and couldn't be approached figuratively without taking as long in improvisation as it would have taken in real life. The problem here was how to provide for the actress that sense of tedium within the character. The job was ritualised into sorting into alphabetical order thousands of pages torn from telephone directories. With *Who's Who,* the cast simulated the running of a stockbroker's office in order to understand the financial world of the City in which most of the characters worked.

Rituals and simulations are only brought into rehearsals, however, when the real job can't be done. For the most part everything possible is done to contribute to the sense of reality of the characters' lives. As well as real time being observed, real newspapers are read, real TV programmes watched and real things used in a host of other ways.

An extension of this work on the content of the characters' lives is research. Research takes the actor out of the rehearsal room and into the world from which the character comes. In simple terms, research can mean, for example, finding out about the job the character does. More sophisticatedly, it involves the actor immersing himself in the social atmosphere and locale of the character he is playing.

To find the world of Beverly from *Abigail's Party,* Alison Steadman, whose performance won her two Best Actress awards in 1977, watched the beauty consultants at work in the West End stores 'and they were all telling me how very, very important make-up was in my life.'[11] As part of his research for *The Kiss of Death,* David Threlfall worked with the Co-op Funeral Service in Manchester and with a private firm in Oldham. Eric Allan and Matthew Guinness spent several weeks absorbing 'the structure and discipline' of medicine as part of their preparation for playing doctors in *Babies Grow Old* by talking to doctors and medical students and attending classes at medical school. In their research for *Nuts in May,* Allan lived in a quarry in Dorset for three weeks and Guinness went to work on a farm. For his portrayal of Muhammad in *Goose-Pimples* Antony Sher learned some Arabic in the Jeddah dialect and the programme credits for that play list dozens of organisations to which he referred during the course of research. By contrast, research can involve the actor in little more than, for example, catching up on the reading his character has done or learning to knit.

Research helps the actors to absorb the social milieu of their characters, whether it's the vegetarian fringe of the south London folk scene from which Keith and Candice-Marie are drawn in *Nuts in May* or the work and routines of being a postman which is the background to *Home Sweet Home.* The location work in filming has led to an extension of research, even with the stage plays, of 'improvising during rehearsals in real places'. In *Abigail's Party,* Beverly tells her guests that when she goes to the supermarket she just grabs her 'wheelie', races round and bungs in what she can find while her husband waits in the car. The moment in the play is based on actual experience: Alison Steadman has described shopping in character:

'She simply whizzed around the place making a grab at anything that was convenient – frozen pizza, frozen pies, frozen anything. All she was interested in was slinging everything in a basket and getting him to write a cheque so that she could get home quicker to polish her toenails.'[11]

Similarly, the cast of *Ecstasy* did figurative improvisations in The Old Bell and Biddie Mulligan's, two 'very hairy' Irish pubs in Kilburn in which the National Anthem of the

11.   John Hall, 'Advancing from Beverly's Ills' (interview with Alison Steadman), *Guardian,* 6 March 1979.

Republic is played at closing time. Specific accounts of improvisations in real places make good material for the raconteur. Leigh says there's 'a separate anthology of funny stories about it.' But from the point of view of the creation of a play or film, research in all its forms contributes to great richness and variety of texture. It lays in that sense of authenticity which is so powerful an ingredient in all Leigh's work: the audience really does believe that the characters belong to the world they claim to come from. Research contributes vitally to the actor's belief in the reality of the character he plays and provides him with material which will inform his action in figurative improvisations.

When, in *Goose-Pimples,* the car salesmen, Irving and Vernon, enumerate the virtues of the Mini-Metro, their exchange, rapturously funny, is grounded in careful research in many motor-showrooms and the dialogue crackles with the truthfulness and authentic vigour of real life. In *Home Sweet Home,* June Fish compensates for the absence of excitement, love and colour in her own life by absorbing the language and values of the paperback romances which she reads so avidly. For her, a headache is 'a band of steel pulled tight across my temples' and the mystery of a woman's suffering is something that 'men cannot comprehend'. Her husband similarly expresses himself through received quotations, but his are culled from joke books and the lyrics of pop songs.

Research, for these characters, and for many others, has contributed directly to the text of the work by providing the material for a specific and idiosyncratic style of language and usage. More than this, research emphasises and intensifies the particular cultural and class background of the character in the play or film by giving the actor the opportunity to absorb into his behaviour and consciousness the economic, social and personal aspects of the field he's researching. There's nothing mysterious about the way this happens; it's what you would expect from acting which is based on specific first hand observation of work, money, leisure and recreation, taste and physical environment. Since one of the themes which is consistently explored in Leigh's work is the way in which people in their behaviour and relationships are limited by the physical and emotional circumstances of their lives, it is entirely natural that the rehearsal process will explore the outer material world of the characters as fully as their inner motivations.

There is one further aspect to research which is implicit in much of what has already been said about it, but which ought not to be overlooked. A fairly common and grudging observation about Leigh's work is that since the actors base their characters on people they know, it follows that his range is always limited by the observations and perceptions of the actors and he doesn't therefore have the imaginative sweep and penetration of the conventional playwright. I find this a doubtful proposition with regard to Leigh's plays and films, but it raises a serious point. Indeed, Leigh's own judgment on most of Cassavetes' films, with the exception of *Shadows* is that they don't work because the improvisations are 'hidebound by the limitations of the actors' experience' in that they simply play themselves. In the context of this discussion research may be seen as an area of sub-textural study for the actor which serves directly to enable him to overcome any such limitations and thus to extend his own experience in the cause of giving increased breadth and depth to both character and characterisation.

There is one exercise in the narrative field which Leigh does apply systematically. 'It's one of the few things I always do' and it brings all the actors together to answer hundreds and hundreds of questions which he puts to them. He calls it the 'Quiz Club', after a lady at Speakers' Corner in Hyde Park who used to wear a little cap on which were inscribed the letters HPQC which stood for Hyde Park Quiz Club. She used to stand on an orange box with an exercise book and she used to shout out, 'Next question: When was the Battle of Trafalgar?' or whatever it was. Someone would say eighteen-something and she'd say, 'No. Wrong. Go to the back.'

Leigh's Quiz Club lasts a day and sometimes longer. (Occasionally, if he's pushed for time, less.) The actors are not to answer the questions out loud, although characters who share a common past or common information may confer if the need arises. The questions usually begin by consolidating information which already exists. For example, he might ask, 'What's your full name? What's your date of birth? Who were your parents? Where did you go to school?' As it progresses,

> I get into saying things like, 'Decide what the following things mean to your character: a helicopter, Karl Marx, Minnehaha etc.' random things which cover the entire spectrum of art, literature, culture, popular culture, politics, geography, travel, domestic things, sexual things, medical things, anything you care to mention.

Some questions consolidate the character's subjective experience – 'What's your first memory of a room you slept in?' – others extend outwards the frame of reference of the character.

The purpose of the activity is to solidify what is already there and also to 'fill in holes', because no matter how thoroughly the characters have been investigated there are inevitably gaps where things have never been discussed or thought about.

> You may, for example, never have discussed whether a character had an operation. With one character it might have been discussed endlessly, but with another it might never have cropped up.

The Quiz Club happens later on in pre-rehearsal when the characters have already 'gelled' so that the actors have the conviction to respond to the questions 'more than arbitrarily', but early enough for the subsequent figurative improvisations to be 'enriched' by what it's stirred up. Once the Quiz Club has happened 'the quality of the substance of the work goes up.' Conversation is 'eased' in the improvisations because the actors have access to a wider range of subjective and factual material.

In following through an account of the ways in which narrative content is explored, stimulated and enriched, I have separated it, unnaturally, but for the sake of clarity, from the other main element of pre-rehearsals which is concerned with the characters' behaviour.

The whole of the first phase of pre-rehearsal is devoted to helping the actor to make the character as real and believable as possible. A detailed biography is created to which is soon added, through figurative improvisation, actual experience of the character's life. Because, at this stage, Leigh doesn't know what the play is going to be about, he can't isolate any one particular area of the character to explore in detail, and consequently everything has to be explored in detail – what the character feels, what he thinks, how he lives, what he eats, where he works, who he knows, and so on. As this exploration progresses the actor's belief in the character is likely to intensify and in this intensity of belief, which is after all the purpose of the work at this point, there is, paradoxically, a possible obstacle to be surmounted. For it has to be pointed out to the actor that, after all, what is being created is not a real human being, but a character who is to appear in a play. Not a person, but an artefact.

The character doesn't exist as an idea or as words in a script. The character is what the actor actually does. So in parallel with all the narrative content, we have to find out how the actor is to play the character.

The character will be played not in response to a few generalised ideas such as 'old', 'grumpy' or 'self-pitying', but 'as a collection of things to be investigated'. In a 'naive form' what there is to be investigated may be 'accent, posture or walk'. On a more sophisticated level subjects may embrace 'terminology and consciousness'.

The exploration of how to play the character takes the rehearsals into an area of some complexity. There is the work of the individual actor to be considered, then the work of the group of actors and finally the way in which everything determines and is determined by the nature of the finished play.

As far as Leigh's work with the individual actor is concerned,

there are ways and means which have evolved over the years of stimulating, amplifying and of bringing things out in the acting which are mainly in two territories: one is the behavioural characteristics of the character and the second is simply the consciousness of the character.

These two facets of the characterisation 'are on the anvil for a great long while' and will bring about enormous changes in the way the actor plays the character. These shifts and alterations in behaviour and consciousness happen 'in parallel with what's going on while the actor is actually being the character in the improvisations'. So, in the narrative, figurative sequence of events, it's likely that:

If I'm playing character A, and you're playing character B, my experience of your character on Monday, week two, will be of such and such a specific quality. But a week later, my experience of your character is totally different. It's a different person. He talks in a different way. He may even talk in a different accent.

Yet against these changes must be balanced the other actors' needs to maintain their belief in the collective reality of the improvisations as a chronological series of events which have actually taken place.

There is clearly the necessity here for an accommodation of each other's work which goes far beyond what is required of most actors in the conventional rehearsals of a scripted play. In a scripted play, to be sure, the actor will probably be encouraged to explore text, characterisation and role in a number of different ways, but always within the bounds of what the script makes possible and usually with reference to the particular line of interpretation being explored in the production. There are no such limitations here. Furthermore, since there is no play, the significance of a change in the character or a series of changes in all the characters, may not become immediately apparent. An actor, for example, who is concentrating on investigating the way in which his character walks is not doing so with any pre-determined result in mind. He might, therefore, discover, with reference back to the original source, that the way of walking is more than just a manifestation of the character's habits of movement, but an expression of some kind of tension, anxiety, even of neurosis. Perhaps this can't be pinned down and needs further exploration. All this will be going on and setting up its own reactions within the other characters in the improvisation – unless Leigh has said that it's to be ignored – without anyone's really knowing what it means. And it's also possible in this case, that at the end of the day it doesn't mean much and has to be rejected.

Another interrelated factor is the extent to which these changes in behaviour and consciousness of characters influence and are influenced by Leigh's own notion of style. The characters in *Goose-Pimples*, for example, are wrought quite differently from those in *Hard Labour*. This isn't just a simple matter of their being different people who would behave differently anyway. The two sets of characters are actually imagined differently. The *Goose-Pimples* people embody the grotesque quality of the play itself. They aspire to sleekness and an abrasive, no-nonsense sophistication, but are undercut by whining speech and a plethora of idiosyncratic behavioural mannerisms and nervous gestures. By contrast, the people in *Hard Labour* are viewed with such microscopic intensity that their very ordinariness appears to have been distilled.

If this variety of tensions and pressures suggests a rehearsal process teetering on the edge of anarchy and flux, the structural discipline which makes it productive is the underlying creative principle discussed above: 'what you do next is in response to what you've already done'. In other words, just as the work on narrative involves the selection and exploration of further possibilities from the firm base of a reality which has already been established, the work on the characters' behaviour is always an extension of what already exists, even if what it brings out is something startling and new.

The characterisations can be directed through means which are themselves figurative and real, or schematic and abstracted. In a figurative exercise, for example, an actor might be asked to play his character, who is normally lively, bright-eyed, wide awake and ebullient, as tired to the point of fatigue on a particular occasion. He is then asked to sustain the character in an improvisation in that state of exhaustion. After a period of playing the character in this way the actor may play the character from then on as always tired. Changes may be effected, too, simply through the character's experience of other people in figurative work. A character, for example, who began life as a cheerful extrovert might become hostile and introverted by virtue of the situations in which he finds himself with other characters and the way in which they treat him.

A handy bit of jargon, which has evolved over the years, and which Leigh uses to identify for the actors the nature of the changes which are being brought about in their characters, is what he calls a character's 'Running Condition'. This may be defined as the character's essential inner tempo reflected in all facets of his behaviour. A change in Running Conditions liberates changes in the actor's way of playing the character's behaviour. The actor who in the above example moved his character from ebullience to fatigue, effects an enormous change in the Running Condition. Where changes are brought about by more abstracted means, Leigh will often make a distinction for the actor between 'the impulse to do an action and actually doing the action'. He makes this distinction clear by describing impulse and action in terms of a flywheel in a machine. The flywheel, which is the impulse, is always there, whirring around; the moments at which it occasionally engages are the actions. Thus, for example, an actor who is playing a 'settled' character might be taken through the following exercise. He is asked to sit in a chair, out of character, and to read the paper. Occasionally he is to move to another chair. The exercise will be set up in an 'abstracted space' and not in any of the real rooms of the figurative improvisations. He's then asked to move to another chair, then another and to keep on changing chairs. Once the principle of the exercise is established out of character, the actor goes into character and is asked to 'find the impulse for him to move to another chair;

find the way for him to do that unconsciously; find the way he never settles.' Find the way, in other words, in which the flywheel impulse is constantly engaging and then sustain that impulse. 'If this works you've dislodged the settled thing and created a new Running Condition.'

When Matthew Guinness was creating the character of Charles in *Babies Grow Old* he was asked to walk around the rehearsal room out of character, punching out at things around the room from time to time. Then, in character, he was asked to find the way in which his character would do the same thing. This impulse was then sustained and explored in the figurative work which followed. It not only quickened the tempo of the character, but gave rise to a compelling gesture of anxiety: the punching of one hand into the other in a subconscious expression of neurotic energy.

In the play, Charles, a doctor, is on the rack of his own conscience. Unable to believe in himself as a GP – 'What are we doing – just prolonging suffering in order to make money for the drug companies?' – he lurches from the public contemplation of suicide to small talk about cooking and cakes. His anger and self loathing are whipped into a poisonous stew of which the other ingredients are envy, impotence and the compulsion to appear respectable and in control of himself. He is a physician who urgently needs healing. The essential condition of the character's inner desperation was made manifest not only in the way the audience learned about his circumstances and problems, but in the whole manner of the physical characterisation, in the rapid staccato of his frequently inarticulate speech, in the spasmodic quality of his attention, in the cartwheel flailing of his arms and in the punching gesture I've just described. Although a similar investigation of any other Leigh character would serve, the example of Charles illustrates Leigh's purposes in the exploration of all aspects of characterisation. His intention is always to find a way to 'heighten the essence of what a character is about'. In this respect his work is close to the art of caricature.

Caricature tends to be viewed as unsuitable territory for serious artists because of its present day associations with journalism and the ephemeral quality of news. In his biography of Gillray, however, Draper Hill provides a perspective which is closer to the heart of Leigh's approach.

Strictly speaking, caricature is not a synonym for satire, or even a genre of drawing. It is a language of exaggeration, a method of projecting inner characteristics, real or imagined, into appearances . . . Caricature is the effort to distil an essence of personality.[12]

It is precisely this 'effort to distil an essence of personality' which engages Leigh in all the work on both narrative and behaiour described so far, and which continues to engage him when he assembles the finished work.

Where he's working specifically on the behavioural dimension of the characters, an exploration of Running Condition is only one of the means at his disposal. He is as likely to spend a long time on purely physical work, finding out more about and developing the ways in which characters walk, how they swing their arms, how they sit, how their posture affects the physical attitude of their heads and so on. When Stephen Rea, whom Leigh describes as 'a wiry, sensitive actor', played Mick, the building labourer, in *Ecstasy*, 'the whole character was released' after a great deal of exploration of the character's physical being. Leigh and Rea worked first on the character's hands and then on how the use of the hands expressed itself throughout the rest of the body until a heavy, lumbering walk was discovered which worked its

12. *Mr Gillray the Caricaturist*, Phaidon, 1965.

way through into all the character's movement and eventually into the whole way in which Rea played the character. Similarly, a lot of solo work may be done on the character's voice (by which I mean timbre, accent, speech pattern and dialect) or on any other physical, social, psychological or emotional aspect of the character which Leigh wants to investigate.

It's plain to see why Leigh has expressed his preference for working with experienced character actors in the light of all this, because it's an area of work which requires great technical accomplishment and skill.

Although I've discussed the two main elements of pre-rehearsal separately, they are not in fact separate at all. They are two layers of the same process, rather than two processes going on side by side. For work on narrative content flows into characterisation; characterisation will stimulate narrative content and, by the same token, research will inform and amplify all aspects of each. The process is fluid, particular and unpredictable.

Creative freedom always implies discipline. The primary discipline of Leigh's work is that whatever is undertaken in rehearsal should always be consonant with the framework of the greater reality which is being explored. Within this general principle, there are a number of specific conventions which govern the improvisations themselves and which embody other creative principles which make productive work possible. The first of these, which I've already referred to, is that the actors should not talk to each other about their characters. The others which I list here should not be seen as a set of rules, prominently displayed to discourage backsliding, but as foundations which support the whole enterprise.

1 Sustaining the improvisation

From the outset the actor is told that he is not to come out of character until instructed to do so. Since he is being asked to apply his fullest concentration to the task it makes good sense not to allow him to set his own limits on his efforts. But, more important, he's encouraged to sustain the character even in those moments of rehearsal when things aren't working. This is because while things aren't working at one moment, they might well be working at the next. More important still, when the actor is in an improvisation with others although things might not be going well for him, they might be for everyone else. Were the actor unilaterally to come out of character in these circumstances he'd cut across other people's work and a creative opportunity might be lost. For these reasons the sustaining of the improvisation is a fundamental discipline of Leigh's rehearsals.

2 Setting up exercises

As a general rule, when Leigh sets up an exercise he does not explain it; he simply asks the actor to do it, out of character at first, so that the principle of the exercise is established, and then to do it in character. If we take, as an example, one of the exercises already described the reasons for this convention should become clear.

The purpose of the exercise in which one character move chairs around in obedience to the peremptory orders of another was to disrupt in some way the cosy atmosphere of that particular relationship. To describe the exercise fully to the actors would be either to imply this purpose, or to make it explicit. Once the actors know what a particular exercise is being used for they're most likely to try to be helpful and deliver the goods, even though they're working in character. This would be unsatisfactory on a number of counts. It's primarily a violation of the reality, because the actors are working as actors to an end which is not consistent with their characters' motivation at that point.

There's a subtle but crucial distinction to be made here because the very aim of this exercise *is* to generate material which runs counter to their motivation. The distinction resides in whether discoveries are made at an unconscious level or whether they are consciously contrived. Working towards a pre-determined end encourages the actor to keep his eye on the target and to head for it. The possibility of unconscious discovery is reduced. If the principle of the activity is established without the actor knowing what it's for, the problem is eliminated.

Leigh's not describing exercises is consistent with every other element of his practice: the work is kept as open-ended as it can be in order to accommodate the greatest number of possibilities. Similarly, to demonstrate an exercise (which is a way of describing it without describing it) makes the activity concrete and practical as opposed to vague and theoretical. Exercises are tools to be used, not concepts to be defined.

3 The actors are not to invent information

Anyone who's ever tried to run an improvisation session knows the deadening, blocking effect that the spontaneous invention of information has on the work. For example, A and B are improvising a conversation between two people at a bus stop.

A: Hello, dear.

B: Hello, er, Mrs Wainwright.

A *didn't know she was called Mrs Wainwright. Neither of course, did B, until the words left her lips.*

A: I like your new hat.

B *isn't wearing a hat. She touches her head, nevertheless, and tries not to let the side down.*

B: Yes.

A: Oh, look at that!

B, *without a clue about what she's supposed to be looking at, gazes vaguely in the direction of A's gesture.*

B: Oh yes!

Pause. B's a bit stuck.

B (*suddenly*): Oh, didn't I see you with your brother last week?

A *doesn't know she has a brother and doesn't know within the context of this improvisation when last week was.*

A: Did you?

I exaggerate, of course, but not by much. There are circumstances when, as a theatre game, it might be useful to run an improvisation where the actors have to accept whatever information they're given in the interests of developing their spontaneity or acceptance, but where an improvisation is an investigation of content – in this case a conversation at a bus stop – this will kill it stone dead. In any case, it's the kind of exercise which would never be used in Leigh's rehearsal because the skills it's supposed to develop can already be taken for granted in the actors he works with. If A and B in my example are playing the exercise as a theatre game, good luck. But if their improvisation has been set up with thorough given circumstances then they're hopeless, because they're undercutting each other's work all the time and introducing elements which aren't only irrelevant but also evasive. The information which is being invented is getting in the way of anything they might be exploring.

In Leigh's work the invention of information would be catastrophic. The invention of non-existent names, invisible articles of clothing, unspecified off-stage events and hypothetical times and relationships would violate the collective reality and block the work. Since, with the background of his characters, there are given circumstances in abundance, the unilateral invention of new information would represent a crass intrusion on carefully prepared work.

4 Notes

Although Leigh keeps copious notes at the stage when he's talking to the actors about the people on their lists, he keeps no improvisation notes and he positively discourages the actors from doing so. His principle is that 'it only exists if you remember it'. Since the characters are growing and changing all the time during pre-rehearsals as a result of their experiences in the improvisations there seems little point in the actors keeping notes on what happens day to day. In any case, the whole essence of the work is that they should remember the characters' world in character. 'It must be in their heads and not on paper.' Actors do keep research notes, though, because if they didn't some important information might get overlooked.

5 Objectivity

I've already referred to the fact that the challenges facing the actor are not the same as the problems and particular experience of the character. For fundamentally practical reasons, therefore, the analysis of an improvisation with each actor is based on a clear distinction between what happens to him and what happened to the character. The actor's objective stance towards his character is fostered and encouraged throughout the process.

There are other reasons why the actor's objectivity is a crucial element in Leigh's work. If the actors worked in a perpetual confusion of first-person perception the result could easily become a kind of psychological soup. The awareness that the character is 'an artefact', 'a fiction' and 'only acting' is kept at the forefront of everyone's mind because it's so important 'that the actor doesn't think it's him'. Objectivity is a corrective to any potential personal disorientation which might come from the actor's intense identification with another person. In an extreme form such disorientation might become psychologically disruptive; in any form a confusion between the actor and the character will inhibit the work.

Leigh cites the example of an actress who was rehearsing an improvised play with another director. In improvisation, her character had a row with a fellow actor's character. At the end of the improvisation the actress said, 'If he does that again, I'm not working with him'. The distinction between what was happening between the characters and what was happening with the actors was so confused in her mind that much of the work was invalidated.

Although usually actors don't have to involve themselves in the content of the play, there have been a number of instances when the nature of the particular piece has demanded that they have been able to take a more general view of its action and ideas than is consistent with the specific perspective of their own characters. In the case of *Babies Grow Old*, for example, the cast had to examine 'all sorts of aspects of the problems of being a GP' and, by implication, touched on the very issues which the play was about. The research, discussion and argument which the work entailed could be profitable only if the actors were able to maintain the distinction between their own ideas and conclusions and the thoughts of the characters they were playing.

With *Ecstasy*, a great deal of time was spent in the pre-rehearsals in investigating the lives of the characters in 1971. Jean, a character played by Sheila Kelley, was a good time girl living for the easy, instant pleasures of drink and sex. Leigh decided, however, that the play itself would be set in the present day, 1979, and that it would be about Jean's dilemma. But he didn't know where Jean would be living in 1979 and without knowing that, the set couldn't be designed. It was necessary, therefore, to investigate with the actress what had happened to Jean in the intervening eight years, as the fun went out of her life and as she was increasingly exploited by men. For this practical reason Sheila Kelley knew what the play was going to be about, even though, when she went back into rehearsal, the improvisations picked up again where they had left off in 1971. Work of this nature simply could not have been undertaken without an actress who was detached from, and therefore in control of, her character.

Another dimension altogether of the actor's objectivity is the way Leigh's plays work in performance. (And the way the performances work in his films.) In a perceptive review of Leigh's work, James Fenton observed that there is 'a sense of aesthetic distance between the spectator and the actor'[13] which he attributed to the combined effect of the characters' minutely observed idiosyncratic mannerisms. Marina Warner touched on it, too, when she described the effect of watching a Leigh play as 'chilly'.[14] The last two lines of Brecht's poem, 'Understanding', which, it's been suggested, 'have the force of a motto for Brechtian actors', provide a key for the understanding of the sensations we experience while watching a Leigh play or film:

These people understand what they are doing so they are understood.[15]

The actor's control of all the material for his character – its social and economic circumstances as well as its psychological and emotional inner life and its behaviour – and his objective command of the dynamic fusion of all these elements, contribute to the capacity for the role to be performed in meticulous detail and with faultless verisimilitude, but without what Brecht identified as the actor's enemy, empathy. There is no confusion for the audience between what it experiences and what the actor is experiencing.

Eventually the pre-rehearsals come to an end. Exactly when they end depends upon the length of the entire process from first rehearsal either to first night or to the beginning of shooting; it's not simply a matter of Leigh's deciding that they've generated enough material from which to make a play. His method of exploration tailors itself to the time allowed by circumstances and by the production company. One of the stage plays, for example, *The Silent Majority*, was virtually thrown together in six days to fill a hole in the Bush Theatre's programme.

It doesn't take long to set up some characters and arrive at a premise from which you can make a simple play – the longer the rehearsals, the more potentially complex the play.

13. 'Comedies of Bad Manners', *Sunday Times*, 29 March 1981.

14. *Critics' Forum*, BBC Radio 3, 14 March 1981.

15. Jan Needle and Peter Thompson, *Brecht*, Basil Blackwell, 1981.

But thirteen weeks rehearsal is 'beginning to be the average for stage plays of any complexity', with six weeks of that spent in pre-rehearsal. He budgets for at least eight weeks of pre-rehearsal before he begins shooting a film. Generally speaking, his earlier work was rehearsed in less time than is now the case. The original Open Space production of *Bleak Moments* was rehearsed in two and a half weeks, as was *Wholesome Glory*. *Babies Grow Old* was the first stage play to have anything like the time he now gets: it was rehearsed in ten weeks.

At the end of pre-rehearsals he writes a scenario which is to be the basis of the next phase of the work, structuring the play. Structuring from the scenario, however, is not just the knocking into shape of the material which has been generated in pre-rehearsal. The scenario *might* follow the narrative events of pre-rehearsal very closely, and equally it might not. The as yet unbroadcast radio play, *Too Much of a Good Thing,* was made by rendering into a clear narrative structure what had happened before, whereas the action of *Abigail's Party* was composed of 'a little of what had happened in pre-rehearsal and a great deal of what I thought ought to happen'. In *Bleak Moments,* the tortuous love scene in which Peter and Sylvia fail to connect was based on fourteen similar occasions in the pre-rehearsals including one where they had sex. The scenario, then, will most often include a great deal of new material, although by its very nature this material must involve the characters in action which is consistent with their existing motivations or can be feasibly motivated out of that which has gone before.

Because the pre-rehearsal period has not been concerned with form, and the scenario *is* form-orientated, the action described in the scenario represents a compression and distillation of themes, ideas and sometimes actual events from the earlier work. The scenarios are always very brief, though, and there's no literary dimension to them. They often consist of no more than headings for scenes and create a rough structure of action on which the play is to be built. The structure is presented to the cast and the work of 'applying a structure' to the improvisation begins.

While there are no fundamental differences of principle in the way Leigh structures a stage play from the way he applies structure to a film, there are considerable practical differences. Once more in the interests of clarity, I will separate the two processes, and examine the work from the point of view of the stage play to show the principles and then deal more briefly with the practical matter of structuring for film. There are three phases in structuring a play. First there is the rough assembly where 'a decent through line' is established for each of the characters but where there is 'no fussing over details'. Next comes the second draft, where the details are examined and challenged. The final phase consists of 'editing, tightening and clarification'.

Before work on the rough assembly can begin another period of realignment might be necessary. Leigh's plays are always set in the present day; that is, the events shown in the play are taken to be happening in the year in which the play's made. The pre-rehearsals, however, might have been based in an entirely different time and sometimes with more than one convention of time going on if groups of characters have been rehearsed separately – although this is more usual in film rehearsals. The fictional time scale of pre-rehearsals can be extremely variable, with the six weeks investigation of the characters representing, in fact, six weeks, or two years, or a week or two days. Thus it's possible to have, for example, 'a perfect character who's twenty-six except that he's twenty-six in 1962'. The synchronising job which is done at this stage might be difficult, but it's essential that it's done.

It has to happen because when it comes to your play or your film, you can't bodge it. You still want to improvise and have improvisations going on which are the richest and most complex and have the least number of flaws in them. This is when you're actually getting the subject matter of the play.

It would obviously save a great deal of time and trouble if the characters could be perfectly aligned from the word go, but, of course, it can't work like that. Characters are selected from the actors' lists in the first place, because of their inherent interest or because something about one of them strikes a spark of possibility off another. Factors such as whether they will conveniently fit each others' chronology do not determine the selection at this stage. Similarly, time cannot be manipulated in the pre-rehearsals with structuring in view. If the work begins to yield an area of narrative content which is concentrated into a sequence of intensely interesting moments in a single evening, it's essential that the time convention is maintained to make further investigation possible. In the example I gave above of the row between the characters Alan, Bob and Chris, the dramatic potential lies in following through the repercussions of the event in the minutest detail, even if it takes two weeks of rehearsal time to improvise a day and a half in their relationship. If Alan, Bob and Chris are only one half of the rehearsal group, it could be that Elizabeth and Frances, who are to be in the same play, but are rehearsing separately, embark upon a sequence of narrative which takes the passage of fictional year to explore. The way in which time is absorbed into the content of the narrative cannot be legislated. Things take as long as they take, but in the structuring of the play there can be no wrinkles, and so before structuring there's often an 'awful phase of melting it all together'.

Where it might be thought that structuring implies a more rigid mode of rehearsal, dominated by the actors' self-conscious awareness of form, it is, in reality, approached in the same spirit of open-ended discovery as the rest of the work. The actors are told, 'Forget we're structuring, this is an improvisation', and the convention underlying the improvisations is still that each event is unique and real. It differs from the figurative work of pre-rehearsal in one respect. It is 'liberated from the strict rules of chronology'. Instead of unfolding in a progressive, chronological way the improvisations can now begin from the same point. To give another fictitious example, a scene heading in the scenario, which says 'John visits Jill and they spend the evening together', encapsulates an event which might be explored dozens of times.

Spending the evening together is not in itself an action, but the total of possibly hundreds of actions, each of which may be investigated. If the very first moments of the evening are broken down, they might appear something like this:

John knocks at the door.
Jill goes to the mirror to check her hair.
Jill opens the door.
They greet each other.
Jill invites him to sit down.
She asks him what he wants to drink.
He decides to have a gin and tonic.
She pours his drink and gives it to him.
She sits down.
He tells her how hard it was to find the house etc.

Each of these individual actions may be explored through improvisation as an event in its own right, or a sequence of them may be run together or, yet again, each action may be broken down into its own constituent actions. When Jill looks in the mirror, for example, is she pleased with what she sees? Does she brush her hair, or comb it?

Where does she keep her brushes and combs? How long does it take? Does she keep John waiting? How long will he wait before he knocks again? Is she anxious about keeping him waiting? Is it deliberate? And so on. All these questions represent material for investigation through improvisation. While repetition will accumulate whole passages of action and dialogue which are the same every time, it's possible to modify other passages or to explore nuances by finding a different emphasis in the characters' motivation or by shifting the focus of their objectives on each occasion the sequence is repeated.

Leigh's principle in keeping the structuring process as open-ended and free as the pre-rehearsal work is to avoid closing down on his options too soon:

> The minute you start to pin it down you start to spot where things can be better, where things can be tightened up. As a writer, you must challenge every moment.

Improvisation is such a spontaneous medium that the material of the play may be challenged in all sorts of unexpected ways, even by external or accidental circumstances. Characters having tea together, for example, might be taken into new areas by one of them choking on a piece of biscuit. A door slamming on the set might take a character's attention off one thing and onto another so that he will see something which he might not otherwise have seen and will, in consequence, launch a new phase of action. The actors will react to such accidental occurrences in character, and the content of each moment will therefore be determined by their motivation, so these occasions have the potential to be dramatically fruitful. In the example of John and Jill, a carefully set-up structuring improvisation may unearth a whole new area of narrative material worthy of further exploration by virtue of John, say, unexpectedly spilling his drink or Jill suddenly finding that the top of the gin bottle's stuck.

In addition to working through the events outlined in his scenario, Leigh will often set up improvisations isolated from the convention of its sequence, the purpose of which is usually to overlay one moment's tension with another in order to make it more dense. A practical example of what this means at its simplest occurs in the first act of *Abigail's Party*. There is a moment at which Laurence puts on a record. In the preparatory improvisations there was a pause here while the characters waited for the music. There was nothing awkward or hollow about it, but Leigh decided that it could be filled in and the moment rendered into a more dense experience for the audience. A parallel improvisation was initiated in which Beverly and Angela admired the fibre-light on the coffee table. The dialogue distilled from this improvisation was then overlaid onto the moment at which Laurence puts on the record.

On a more complex level, a couple of actions from John and Jill's first few minutes together might be looked at in isolation from the overall sequence of which they're a part. The way in which Jill pours and mixes drinks can be investigated in its own right. Perhaps John smokes, in which case the particular manner in which he gets out his cigarettes and lights one can be explored. Then, a conversation which may or may not have happened in pre-rehearsal, about some topic which is totally unrelated either to drinking or smoking may be improvised by itself and further explored. And finally all three events are laid on top of each other within the context of the master narrative. So what appeared in the breakdown of action, given as part of this example, as 'She pours his drink and gives it to him', might become, in the play, a little sequence in which Jill clumsily pours drinks while John fumbles for his cigarettes and the two of them talk about the number of farms there are on the Duke of Norfolk's estate.

This rehearsal procedure of isolating improvisations from the narrative sequence gives him access to dramatic devices which enhance the texture of the play's surface.

It also makes it possible for him to create moments which, in the normal run of things, might not naturally occur in figurative work. It could be, for instance, that while John and Jill had, in one improvisation, talked about the Duke of Norfolk, they would be extremely unlikely to broach the topic at the moment of pouring the drinks. As long as it squares with the characters' motivation, such a thing can be contrived to happen in the cause of dramatic interest. The extent to which Leigh will bring together a number of diverse elements in one moment depends entirely on the style of the particular play, on 'how naturalistic I want it'.

The scenario embodies the dramatic material of the play. The conflicts and emotional tensions, the pressures on the characters and the heightening of the material are what's being investigated in the application of structure and each improvisation is an exploration for Leigh of the most effective, powerful, rich and condensed way of expressing all these in dramatic terms while at the same time intensifying and remaining true to the characters' natures and motivation. When each scene has been thoroughly investigated in this manner the rough assembly stage is complete. Altough he says that details aren't to be fussed over, it is an immensely detailed phase of the work. And since the substance throughout is the inner drives of the characters, it isn't that rough at all.

The next phase of structuring is to go over all the material again and challenge it moment by moment. Once again, although many areas of the play will have been set by the work on the rough-cut, Leigh still keeps the doors open for new and better material to be incorporated and for previously fixed material to be discarded, until

> finally you're into discussions about who moves where and who says what and which words should be swapped round in the word order and which lines should be rewritten because there's a repetition and which adjective should be replaced by another one because it's unsonorous or too alliterative – ordinary writing considerations.

In essence, the process of arriving at a play is one of refining each pulse of action until what is reached is a text without a script. While Leigh's plays are frequently referred to as 'improvised plays' there is no improvisation or spontaneous invention of dialogue in performance. As he's often had to make clear he's 'not interested in Happenings'. There have been moments in two of the films where a scene has been shot in which the dialogue has been 'improvised without a structure'. In the case of the dinner party scene in *Who's Who*, there wasn't time to structure it, and in *Grown-Ups* Brenda Blethyn was allowed to 'kind of improvise' Gloria's breakdown because the scene was so emotional. In both instances there was the possibility of re-shooting and finally of editing to get it right. But of all the stage plays, Matthew Guinness's final speech as Charles in *Babies Grow Old* marks the only occasion that an actor has embarked on a speech in performance without knowing precisely what he was going to say. Even this speech was only 'left a bit loose at the edges' and then, because it sprang from such intensity of feeling that the number of times the character exclaimed 'Gosh!' was unpredictable.

It's only since *Abigail's Party* that Leigh's plays have been written down at all. No one needs a script –

> because, and this is the real principle of the thing, the characters, the motivations, the objectives, and all the other contingent elements make an actor so well informed about it all that he remembers what it's all about.

When Sam Kelly was asked how acting of such sensitivity could withstand the rough and tumble of filming, where there are all the constituent elements of a film unit on location as well as other distractions, he replied that in Leigh's work the actor is stronger and tougher than is usually the case in filming because of the depth and detail which the work has achieved.

The character is conceived in solitary improvisation and is not brought into contact with any other until the actor is able to sustain the character, alone, with nothing going on. These origins are recalled in the preparations for stage performance. The actors are called to the theatre ninety minutes before curtain up, and a considerable part of this time is spent simply getting into character and sustaining it. With filming, the instruction to the actors 'warm up' is added to the customary cues for the unit, 'Sound . . . Camera . . . Action!' and it's a sign to the entire working group for silence so that the actor can get into character before shooting begins.

Films are structured on the same principles as the stage plays but with practical differences related to the specific demands and possibilities of the medium. With the play, 'the sequence of things is inevitable and has to be adhered to in an obvious way because the actor has got to get from A to Z' while the film narrative can run in a more fluid way, with jumps in time and action.

Although the sequence of action in a film is as thoroughly worked out as for a stage play, the scenes are unlikely to be shot in sequential order and the establishing of the actor's through line is that much trickier. When a film is shot on a scenario 'it will actually say, next to each scene, what day it is: that is what *imaginary* day.' This little procedure is an indication of the measures that are taken to keep the reality alive for the actor in the more fragmented context of filming. The scene is a specific event, taking place on a specific day. But while this convention helps the actor to maintain his sense of time and place, it does not, in the end, govern the way in which the film is edited because 'you can cheat like mad if you want to in the cutting room since there isn't any responsibility to the actor's motivation.' The material can be arranged as Leigh chooses in the editing stage, 'so long as the character's motivation remains coherent from the audience's point of view'.

The greatest practical difference between films and stage plays in the manner of their structuring is that the films are structured during the shooting period and not before. As has already been discussed, the pre-rehearsals are 'for creating the world of the characters,' so 'you're not in a frame of mind for structuring things, then'. Nevertheless, structuring on the spot can involve horrendous risks as is illustrated by the example of how the climax of *Grown-Ups* was found. In spite of the risks, however, the procedure is consistent with the entire philosophy of the work.

> You've got to rehearse and structure on location because the location affects the precise action and dialogue and the rhythms of what happens.

In order for the actors totally to believe in the world of the characters, and for the films, therefore, to breathe that sense of real life which is their principal common characteristic, the work has to be structured in the actual places where it will be shot. While the mornings and afternoons are spent shooting, the evenings are devoted to 'stockpiling and structuring dialogue' for scenes to be shot on the following day. Because it's film, of course, the fine tuning of the composition ultimately takes place in the cutting room, but structuring for films is still very rigorous and thorough because 'the more refined and organised what you shoot, the better the raw material you take to the cutting room'.

In 1961 I went, with the jazz musician Evan Parker, to a lecture on contemporary theatre given by Martin Esslin in Birmingham. At the end of the lecture Parker asked whether Esslin saw any future for improvisation in drama. Now, over twenty years later, his emphatic 'No' seems, to say the least, hollow. I mention this not to score any cheap points off Mr Esslin. Quite the opposite, in fact, because at the time the reasons he gave for his answer made perfect sense and were generally accepted by everyone in his audience. Improvisation could be of value in training and in education, he said, but as far as the formal disciplines of art were concerned, it was altogether too volatile a medium, too unstructured and too loose. Everyone agreed because, then, no one knew any different.

If these ideas have lost their currency, it's almost entirely due to Leigh and is a measure of the originality of his contribution to our theatrical life. Nevertheless, the prejudices and doubts about plays which originate in improvisation have been slow to erode, even though Leigh's influence has been spreading steadily over the years and may be seen in the work of Mike Bradwell and Hull Truck, Les Blair, Sheila Kelley, Sarah Pia Anderson and, most recently, Phil Young. In fact, it was only in his review of Young's *Crystal Clear,* that James Fenton became the first major critic to acknowledge explicitly that 'improvised plays are just as much plays as any other kind'. 'Indeed,' he went on, 'the tendency with improvised plays appears to be towards a much higher degree of accuracy in characterisation than with the average pre-conceived authorial script.'[16] While it may be encouraging to see these remarks as the sign of a great shift in the tide of critical attitudes to Leigh's work, and the work of other deviser directors who use this method, the fact remains that most criticism doesn't seem able to escape from the idea that improvised plays are some kind of curiosity; perhaps not even proper plays at all.

Much of the criticism of Leigh's work is wide of the mark, and sometimes so wide of it as to be insulting. This is because just as his method implicitly challenges some of the most fundamental assumptions about what may be achieved through improvisation, so the plays and films similarly challenge many of our existing ideas of content and style in drama. Leigh's innovations extend far beyond his way of making plays and into the very nature and substance of the dramatic experience.

16. *Sunday Times*, 12 December 1982.

3:APPROACHES TO THE PLAYS & FILMS

In terms of narrative, setting and incident, the scale of Leigh's work is small. Reduced to their storylines his plays and films appear, as he says himself, 'banal'. In *Nuts in May,* a vegetarian couple go on a camping holiday in Dorset and the husband has a fight with a Brummie over the lighting of a campfire; in *The Kiss of Death,* an undertaker's assistant has an uneasy relationship with a girl who works in a shoe shop; in *The Permissive Society,* a lad brings his girl friend back to his council flat on the same evening that his sister is stood up by a man. Even in the works where there are births and deaths – *Babies Grow Old, Hard Labour, The Kiss of Death, Abigail's Party* and *Grown-Ups* – the scale on which they occur is small and domestic. One of the most shocking scenes in Leigh's work (one that is, to which people have reacted with violent shock) occurs in *The Kiss of Death* when the undertakers, Trevor and his boss, Mr Garside, go to fetch the body of a dead baby. The parents are distraught with understated grief. The event is terrible. But the baby has died in a trim little house on a new estate and around the tragedy life goes on. 'What time do you finish?' asks Mr Garside of the policewoman who's in attendance. 'Two o'clock,' she replies. 'You've got all afternoon to yourself then.' he observes while Trevor's at the car fetching the shroud.

With the exception of the character of Charles from *Babies Grow Old,* and of *Who's Who* where the action fans out from the social stratification of a city stockbroker's office to accommodate, at one end, a peer of the realm, and at the other, a lower middle-class clerk, the social range of Leigh's work is confined to working-class or lower middle-class settings. Where foreigners appear, they come rarely as exotic interlopers but as characters whose presence is usually an extension of the class background of the play. Thus, Naseem, the Indian immigrant in *Hard Labour* and Mick, the Irishman in *Ecstasy* clearly belong in the working-class milieu they inhabit. Muhammad, the Arab in *Goose-Pimples* is a bit different. He is in England on a visit and hardly speaks any English. He really doesn't belong, but his presence focuses the class-bound aspirations and blatant prejudices of the other characters.

Leigh's work doesn't bestride the epic ground of plays such as Peter Flannery's *Our Friends in the North,* where the stage throngs with diplomats, politicians and power brokers and the action embraces great tracts of time and geography. The time span of Leigh's action is usually a single evening, a few days or, perhaps, a week or so. *Grown-Ups* covers ten months, but most of the film's action is concentrated into the first couple of weeks of Dick and Mandy's moving in to their new house, and the big leap of time accommodates a brief Christmas-time coda, where we find that Mandy is very close to having her baby. The longest period covered is six years, when in *The Birth of the 2001 FA Cup Final Goalie,* a baby is discussed, conceived and born, grows into a toddler and is eventually seen playing football with his dad. This all happens in the space of five minutes.

Where people travel their journeys are usually no more than a function of their situation. Keith and Candice Marie move around a fair bit in *Nuts in May* but that's because they're on holiday. Mrs Thornley makes short trips by bus to go to work or to see her family in *Hard Labour*. In *Goose-Pimples* Vernon whisks his guest off round the North Circular to buy them a meal, but Beverly's visitors have only come from a few doors away on the evenings of *Abigail's Party*. There is no sweep to these characters' comings and goings.

There is never a heroic dimension in Leigh's work. No one ever sets off to change the world or fight for right or fulfil his destiny. There are no great shifts of attitude or conviction. There are no characters who, through individual action, put everything straight. His central characters are not even heroic by that contemporary inversion which has given us the anti-hero, implacably corrupt, or impotent but raging. Leigh's people mostly just live and cope or fail to cope. There are a few acts of kindness. In *Hard Labour* for example Ann Thornley and Naseem spend the evening in bleak surroundings of a taxi-cab office on the ground floor of a virtually derelict house. Naseem works all the time and they have nowhere else to go. With reference to a friend who's become pregnant, Ann says 'I hope that never happens to me.' 'You are, er, different girl, see.' replies Naseem. 'You have got friend. When you're my friend, see, I am looking after that one, and you don't have this trouble, see.' Ann smiles. The kindnesses are mostly of this scale, coming simply from the goodness of people's hearts, without grandeur.

It's been suggested that the consistency with which Leigh sets his work in this allegedly narrow band of social class and concentrates his attention on minor incidents and 'banal' narrative is in some way an indication of his limitations as a playwright. It's a viewpoint, however, which doesn't stand up to any serious scrutiny. If Leigh's work can be said to be limited on these grounds, then the same charge may be laid at Jane Austen, Chekhov, Philip Larkin and Vermeer; not a bad limited company. There is the example of *Who's Who* to indicate that he's perfectly well able to investigate other levels of society if he chooses, but more to the point is that this 'narrow' band of working-class and lower middle-class society actually includes most people in this country. In other words, it's us: the world of Leigh's plays and films contains multitudes. It's the world we know and its events are things with which we are to a greater or lesser extent familiar.

The characters almost always seem to be people we might conceivably know. This is a difficult point to quantify, but it generally appears to be the case that when people talk about Leigh's plays and films one of the commonest observations is that the characters are very familiar. This could be attributed, in part, to their unremarkable jobs and where they live. Leigh's characters work, for the most part in 'ordinary' jobs: they're postmen, teachers or estate agents for example; local government employees, night-watchmen, domestic cleaners or driving instructors; lots of them work in shops. Apart from Lord Crouchurst in *Who's Who* who lives in Kensington, and the upper-class stockbrokers who have their own up-market addresses, they tend to live modestly, in suburban areas on new estates if they're doing all right; in council houses or rented flats if their means are more slander.

The things they do are also familiar. A lot of eating goes on in Leigh's work; not that all the characters tuck vast amounts away though one or two do, but eating, as an activity, occurs a lot; there's a lot of drinking, too, and, as a natural consequence, a lot of going to the lavatory. Sometimes the body functions less well, for there are a couple of bouts of vomiting and a fair bit of illness. They have a lot of domestic rows and arguments and, without its ever becoming a complete preoccupation, there's a fair amount of sex. The characters smoke a lot and there's a great deal of talk about work, and plenty of examples of work itself. Their lives seem a lot like yours or mine.

The world for most of these characters has material foundations. In *Hard Labour,* the Thornley family are Roman Catholics, but Mrs Thornley's the only one who goes to church. Her religion is of no use to her, though, for she cannot reconcile its notions of spirituality and love with the remorseless drudgery and lack of fulfilment in her material existence. When she confesses her shortcomings – 'I just don't love people enough' – the priest on the other side of the confessional doesn't understand her problems and is impatient to be rid of her so that he can get on with reading the paper.

Without relevant faiths or ideologies, the characters' main concerns are with getting on with their lives through work and social relationships. Here again, the situations they get themselves into are very familiar. When in *Bleak Moments* Peter, having finally plucked up courage to ask Sylvia out, takes her to a virtually empty Chinese restaurant, replete with hostile waiter and a lone, slurping diner, the cinema audience ripples with the sensation of the familiar awfulness and the miserable meal to come. Similar tremors of recognition and anticipation occur frequently in all the plays and films. When, in *Nuts in May,* Keith and Candice Marie return to the campsite to find Ray's transistor playing near their tent, the reverberations of similar holiday confrontations are set up in the viewer, and it's the same when Finger and his girl friend Honky, a couple of exuberant working-class Brummies, career across the field on their motor-bike. When Gloria turns up at Dick and Mandy's house for the third or fourth time with her strident 'Cooo-eee' we can scarcely hold back our reciprocal groans of 'Oh, no!'

As far as work is concerned, for most of the characters it's a necessary evil. They're not lazy backsliders; it's just that their jobs either bring them no fulfilment, or add to their anxieties and frustrations. A few characters do enjoy work, to be sure; the stockbrokers seem to have a good time in *Who's Who.* When Anthony Trotter is asked whether the job's 'fun' he says 'It can be when we make lots of money', but it's an enjoyment which owes everything to the privilege of his birth. Laurence, in *Abigail's Party,* pursues work with a single-mindedness which eventually kills him, and his wife's career as a beauty consultant is echoed in her own obsession with appearances and superficial glamour. The car salesmen in *Goose-Pimples* find some status in their jobs as does Mr Payne in *Too Much of a Good Thing;* he's a rat catcher but prefers to be known as 'a rodent operative'. For these few examples of characters whose engagement with work offers some satisfaction however, there are many more who are completely misplaced in their jobs. The starkest examples occur in *Hard Labour* where the Thornleys are tied to a chain of work. Jim Thornley gets a hard time from his overseer, who, it's clear, is getting a hard time from the 'big wigs from London'. Jim gives his wife a hard time, in turn. Sylvia and Pat in *Bleak Moments* have numbing routine jobs, as do Dick and Mandy in *Grown-Ups.* Their friend, Sharon, is totally dissatisfied. When she's 'on sweets' she'd rather be 'in dresses' and when she eventually gets to dresses she'd 'rather be back on sweets'. Trevor, the undertaker's assistant, working among the dead, seizes the opportunity to affirm life: when he's asked to help an old lady, Mrs Ball, who's fainted on the stairs he cossets her with almost obsessive concern.

Problems with work, problems with relationships, the odd row, the bodily functions, home life and social life; this is the world for most of the characters in Leigh's plays and films. There are no great events, no enormous intrigues, no twists and turns of plot or character. There are stories of mainly small events in the lives of unspectacular and largely unfulfilled people, who neither discuss 'issues' nor stand for significant points of view. Given only the story outlines of the works we might even think of them as the stuff of somewhat drab soap opera, or, more charitably, as tiny social miniatures. The scale, however, is entirely deceptive. The first ingredient of this deception to consider is the way in which the plays and films come to us originally, through the medium of performance.

At the end of *Babies Grow Old* an elderly lady, Mrs Wenlock, struggles to open a put-u-up so that she can go to bed. It's in the living-room, the warmest room in the house. She's surrendered it the night before to her pregnant daughter, Elaine, and her son-in-law, Geoff, a doctor, who have paid her a flying visit. She has slept upstairs in her own freezing bedroom while they have been with her, but now they've left and she's on her own. Mrs Wenlock is ill. Geoff, described as 'unfeeling'[1] and 'careless',[2] has closed the put-u-up before leaving. So Mrs Wenlock struggles with it. And struggles. And, because she's old and dying, continues to struggle, until, unbearably slowly, the lights go down and the play ends. *Babies Grow Old* was performed at the RSC's Other Place in Stratford, and the ICA in the Mall. It would be fair to say that the audiences who saw it were unlikely to be theatrically naive. Many times during those final minutes, members of the audience called out with offers of help. There was no elaborately contrived suspense to account for these responses and no melodramatic situation with a pay-off of the plot. A laconic old lady, played by Anne Dyson, a well known Shakespearian actress, simply struggled to open a put-u-up.

In the third scene of *Ecstasy,* whch played at the Hampstead Theatre, an enraged wife Val, finds Roy, her husband, in the cramped and squalid flat of Jean, the play's central character. Val and Roy have a fight which grows increasingly violent and brutal. Their language is foul; the fight goes on and on and suddenly Jean's bed, on which they're struggling, collapses at one end. The sophisticated London audience gasp and the auditorium buzzes: 'Was that supposed to happen? How are they going to get out of this?' Later, some other characters arrive with the intention of mending the bed. It was supposed to happen.

A group of students have been to see a star-studded classic revival of *The School for Scandal*. It's a production for which they've been unable to muster much enthusiasm. The following morning at nine o'clock we start to watch *Who's Who* on video. They're bright young people and many of them have a sharp, informed interest in contemporary theatre. Within minutes they're squirming in their seats at the behaviour and pretentions of some of the characters, and the room's actually noisy with their comments.

This kind of spontaneous participation in the moment to moment events on stage or screen is unusual in the light of the ordinariness of the situations or the smallness of their scale. The noisy participation of these examples is probably exceptional, but it's a sign of the degree of animation which Leigh's work stirs up in audiences. This is a phenomenon which it is important to look at in some detail.

There's a moment in the wedding service when the priest asks the congregation if there's anyone present who can show grounds why the marriage which is about to be

1. Michael Billington, *Guardian,* 12 December 1982.

2. Benedict Nightingale, *New Statesman,* 21 February 1975.

solemnised should not take place. Most people at most weddings attend precisely because they're certain it will take place; the predictability of the event is emphasised by the predictability of the marriage ritual itself. Nevertheless, at that one moment, the predictability of things is challenged and the uncertainty of real life floods the occasion. Suppose someone does object? What happens then? There can't be many people who have lived through that moment without some sensation of unease, a tightening of the gut, an intensification of attention.

A similar sensation to this may be experienced in the theatre when something goes wrong with a performance, even if the actors try to cover it by ad-libbing. There's an unmistakable sense of things shifting gear as the actors abandon their carefully rehearsed sense of the play's language and rhythm to deal with the unpredictable new situation. It's the same when an actor loses his lines on stage and struggles to retrieve them. The effect of such moments is to switch the attention of audience and actors into a different mode. Suddenly, what's happening on stage is actually real: the play has gone wrong or the man's forgotten his lines; rather than a representation of something real: this man wants to kill his step-father in an act of revenge.

Leigh tells the story of a performance he once saw of a play set in a glass factory. There was a scene in which one of the characters had a heart attack while he and others were working on a large and expensive sheet of plate glass. The glass was represented by a sheet of perspex and the acting was 'convincing' in the bland way that so much acting is. The audience 'registered' the scene but didn't experience it. Shortly afterwards, another of the characters was given a real cut glass bowl to work on. He went over to his chair to start the job, but as he sat down the chair collapsed, unplanned.

> It really collapsed. The bowl jumped out of his hands and he caught it. At that moment there was an electricity in the theatre which had not existed in the previous hour and three-quarters, because suddenly, it really was a glass bowl, it really was a chair breaking and it really was all happening.

This is another example of a sudden, spontaneous event happening on stage which galvanises the attention of everyone present. Leigh's account goes on to offer an analysis.

> What was telling was that he caught it and then smiled at the audience and the audience clapped. So the whole illusion which the thing should have been about was completely shattered because of an embarrassment the actor discovered at having been through this moment of reality. To get himself out of it he had to share it with the audience by completely coming out of the illusion of the play.

The play tells the audience that this character understands glass and works with it well enough to earn his living from it. In the scene with the sheet of plate glass the men must both look to their stricken workmate and save the precious glass. Saving the precious glass is a metaphor, if you like, for the character's work. But when the actor is really called upon to save the precious glass by making sure that the bowl doesn't smash, he is unable to cope with the moment in character. He comes out of character to signal to the audience 'That wasn't supposed to happen and now we'll get on with the play.' The only conclusion one can reach is for that actor in that character the relationship with glass, which is fundamental to the whole world of the play, doesn't actually exist. It has simply been signalled through that elaborate coded convention which is accepted by both actors and audience. (The audience clearly *had* accepted the convention, because they rewarded the actor with a round of applause.) The performance offered not an illusion, but the illusion of an illusion.

Leigh's characters, as the account of the method has demonstrated, do have real relationships with each other and with the things in the material world around them. These relationships exist because they are the actual experiences which shape the character and form the substance of the play. The results of this work for the actor are two-fold; first, he knows so much about the character from these experiences that he is totally secure; and, second, on the basis of this security, he is able to play the character's responses to dramatic events as though they were completely real. Thus, had the man in the glass factory been a character in one of Leigh's plays, his relationship with glass is certainly one strand in his existence which would have been thoroughly researched and investigated. Had the accident with the chair occurred, he would have been able to deal with it in character and intensify the illusion. But it goes further than this. Since in Leigh's work the whole mode of the character's existence is his response to spontaneous events (throughout pre-rehearsal and through most of structuring, remember, the actor in character has not known what's going to happen next) the actor is able to play *everything* that happens to his character as a spontaneous event. In terms of the actor's spontaneity, each moment for the character is invested with the quality of immediacy which Leigh describes in the story of the actor dropping the bowl. The fact that the characters' experience appears to be happening 'now' is an enormously powerful element in Leigh's plays and films. When Jean-Louis Barrault, in his celebrated lecture on theatre to Oxford University said, 'Theatre is . . .', paused as though ill or distracted until the audience was electric with concern, and then finished his sentence, '. . . the art of the present moment', he defined the matter perfectly.

The world for the characters unfolds moment by moment in an unpredictable stream of events and reactions, and it's because of this that the stage or screen performance has the same qualities for the audience; it's this directness of the characters' involvement with their own lives which accounts for the audience's responses to Mrs Wenlock's struggle with the put-u-up, the collapse of Jean's bed and Alan Dixon's toadying contortions. They're apparently happening totally in the present moment. They seem to be real. The audience perceives the performance of Leigh's plays and films in a way which is similar to the congregation's perception of that moment in the wedding service.

Although the scale of the incidents in Leigh's work is small, the audience's perception of them is heightened by the intensity of the moment by moment reality. Material, therefore, which might seem at first to be hopelessly unfruitful for dramatic exploration, becomes rich and engaging. It's more than a device of style, however, for Leigh to create the circumstances in which this manner of involvement is achieved. 'I've always thought,' he says, 'ever since I was a kid, it's always seemed interesting to have in a film or a play things just like everyday life.' It's an interest which has brought him in adult life to a profound appreciation of the painting of Vermeer, whose work he acknowledges as an influence on his own. In the multi-dimensional medium of drama it's developed into a concern with:

. . . putting on the screen or stage people doing things that you don't see in plays. For example, I always thought what a gas it would be if you could go to the pictures and see a couple kissing the way it happens and not the way that people always kiss in movies. And that's what we've got in *Bleak Moments*. It is actually a love scene that's awkward and twitchy with the warts and all going on.[3]

3. Mike Leigh, *Arena*, BBC2 TV, 4 September 1982.

In his review of the film of *Bleak Moments,* the American critic Roger Ebert distinguished between what he calls 'traditional movies' and 'new movies'.

Traditional movies have characters whose titles (hero, cowboy, kid-sister, loser) determine the way they behave. Even the so called Hollywood New Wave Movies (*Five Easy Pieces, The Last Picture Show*) give us characters who act in their own self-image. So we see what they do, and often we're engrossed. But we never seen how they interact with one another – how their behaviour determines their fates.[4]

By contrast, the 'new movies', of which *Bleak Moments* is one, consider 'the ways people really behave toward each other'. They

represent a whole new way of using film. We don't just get the sight of the plot unfolding; we see the process of the plot unfolding. What happens at one instant in the movie really does seem to determine what happens next. This is a new kind of suspense, the suspense of real stories happening in real time.[4]

The qualities which Ebert notes in *Bleak Moments* are common throughout all Leigh's work. While the plays and films undoubtedly tell stories, what's important in them is not the narrative itself, but the 'process' of the narrative. For example, there are several 'boy meets girl' stories. The story of Linda and Trevor in *The Kiss of Death* is even similar in some respects to the story of Sylvia and Peter; Linda, like Sylvia, has to do the chasing and both women's pursuits culminate in a direct sexual invitation to the unwilling man, in scenes which share a tense, unromantic atmosphere and the absence of any whiff of eroticism. Sylvia says to Peter:

I was busy saying something to you in my head. It was quite amusing.
PETER: What?
SYLVIA: I was saying to you . . . take your trousers off. It was a sort of joke, really. I mean in the sense that if we could ever get around to touching one another it wouldn't be a bad thing.
PETER: I don't know what to say.

With Trevor, Linda is less circuitous. 'You can kiss me if you like,' she tells him. Eventually he does. 'Are you coming upstairs?' she asks, 'Come on.' He doesn't move. 'You'd better go then, hadn't ya?' He goes. Regardless of their common features, each of these episodes is quite different, as is the essential nature of each relationship, because of the particularity of the characters. Linda's motivation and behaviour is as uniquely different from Sylvia's as Trevor's is from Peter's. The same sort of things might be happening to the characters but each experiences it in his own singular way.

It's this unique and particular dimension to the way in which the characters experience the unfolding, moment by moment, of their lives which is actually a considerable part of the content of Leigh's work. For no matter what ideas or themes might be explored in any particular play or film, the exploration is accomplished through the minutely detailed observation and representation of the interaction of characters who are, to all intents and purposes, real. It's probably a bit much to suggest that Leigh's work, in the truthfulness of its observation and the minuteness of its detail, celebrates everyday life, because for most of the characters everyday existence is sharp and painful. It's not, however, excessive to say that what is celebrated is the human scale. Above anything else these plays and films are about, to

4. 'Bleak But Beautiful', *Chicago Sun Times,* 1972 (exact date unknown).

use Roger Ebert's phrase, 'the ways people really behave toward each other'.

In *Nuts in May,* Keith and Candice Marie Pratt, holidaying in Dorset to 'be with Mother Nature, and laugh and sing and play', apparently conduct their lives in accordance with the first principle of the human scale: love thy neighbour – or as Keith somewhat more ponderously puts it, 'One should have consideration for one's fellow creatures.' Consequently, they are, by their own lights, polite, law abiding and, in one of Keith's favourite words, 'responsible'. Their sense of responsibility has caused them to construct what they see as a well ordered, well regulated pattern upon their lives. It surfaces in what proves to be a rare moment of contentment on their camping holiday.

CANDICE MARIE: Are we having salad for lunch?
KEITH: That's right.
CANDICE MARIE: What's the treat?
KEITH: Guess.
CANDICE MARIE: Raw mushrooms.
KEITH: That's right.
CANDICE MARIE: My favourite. And onions and nut roast for supper?
KEITH: Boiled jacket potatoes.
BOTH: Vitamin C in their skins.
KEITH: Yoghurt to follow and cocoa at bedtime.
CANDICE MARIE: I'm very happy Keith.
KEITH: Yes, so am I .

Their happiness, however, is built on the flimsiest foundations, for while they are united in their commitment to a style of living which is ecologically pure, they are, in fact, blind to each other's real needs and desires. The first days of their holiday are littered with their minor arguments and bickerings. Keith's view of the world is rational, causal and ordered. He knows the proper geological terms for rock formations, and the Latin names for flowers. He has a schedule for each day of the holiday, which must be adhered to, because 'there's no point in having a schedule if you don't stick to it'. He's also got a maximum-minimum thermometer for measuring the temperature, a portable barometer for measuring the weather, a pedometer for measuring how far they walk, an exercise manual for keeping in shape and a system which governs what they eat and how many times they chew it.

His wife is altogether more romantic. She makes up songs, paints and writes poetry.

CANDICE MARIE: Do you want to hear my new poem, Keith.
KEITH: Yes, I'd love to.
CANDICE MARIE: A gentle flower that grows in spring,
    That feels the sun upon his face,
    That's free to smile and laugh and grin.
    It knows no guilt or hate or sin,
    It has no battles it must win.
    Oh, how I love and envy him.

At Corfe Castle, while her husband hogs the guide book and contemplates 'the great nimbo-cumulus rising above', she's more excited by knowing where the dungeons are and imagining 'what it must have been like hundreds of years ago'.

All the, er, kings and queens walking about in all their fineries . . . And eating great bowls of fruit and luscious grapes, and drinking out of golden goblets, must have been lovely.

She's appalled to think of the ghosts of these figures returning to the castle to find it littered with crisp bags and sweet papers.

CANDICE MARIE: Do you think they do come back, Keith?
KEITH: What?
CANDICE MARIE: Their ghosts.
KEITH: No. There's a car going up the B3351.

In one wonderfully compressed scene, in which action and location fuse into a single metaphor for their relationship, Keith stands on the beach at Lulworth Cove and shouts to Candice Marie on the cliffs above:

You're standing on sedimentary limestone. It's been folded into the shape of a stair, that's why it's called Stair Hole . . . there's a stair there and a hole down there.

From a hundred feet above him, she shouts back, 'I can't hear you Keith.' They are two people failing to connect across a great distance.

For all the self-righteous humanity of their values and ideas, their differences are never resolved. He bullies her into doing what he wants to do and she nags at him until he does what she wants to. Meanwhile, the Dorset in which they're holidaying is peopled by shrewder and more cynical folk than their vapid notions of rural bliss had led them to expect. The campsite proprietor insists on payment in advance, the local farmer from whom they try to buy untreated milk engages them in a discussion of economic reality, and a quarryman is keen to sell them a fossil or two.

The absence of any real connection between their ideas about life, and what life is actually like is most fully exposed in their dealings with the other people on the campsite. With Ray, a PE student on a field trip, Keith becomes jealous because Candice Marie seems to like him in spite of the fact that he plays his radio loud, smokes and takes sugar. With Honky and Finger, the raucous Brumies whom neither like, matters take a violent turn. Finger starts an open fire on which to cook sausages ('You shouldn't be eating sausages.' Keith tells him. 'Apart from the toxic substances in the meat there are quite a few harmful additives and preservatives in the sausage.') Keith assumes responsibility for preventing this breach of the countryside code.

KEITH: Stop what you're doing.
FINGER: No. Look, I've paid my money, you've got no right to come telling me what to do.
KEITH: Oh, I've got every right. I have the power to arrest you if I wanted to, now stop making that fire.
FINGER: Are you a copper?
KEITH: No, but every citizen has the right to arrest another citizen who's breaking the law. Now, be told.

Eventually Keith has to use force. He pursues Finger around the field, wielding a stick and screaming, 'I'll knock your head off'. Then suddenly he bursts into tears and ignoring Candice Marie's attempt to help him, he blunders off into the woods to be on his own.

The Pratts' sanitised love-thy-neighbour philosophy exists only as long as there are no neighbours around to put it to the test. As soon as it is challenged it's revealed, even to Keith, for the prescriptive sham it is; his tears are an acknowledgement of the gulf between his ideals and the reality of human affairs. He cannot accommodate anyone who is different. It might be expected that this insight would be enough to compel him, supported by his wife, to reassess himself, no matter how painful this might be. But the end of *Nuts in May* finds them more firmly entrenched in their previous position than before, even though this signals a yet further retreat from the real world. 'Wouldn't it be lovely, Keith,' fantasises Candice Marie, 'if we were gypsies like in the old days. And we had a lovely painted caravan and we could stop wherever we wanted.'

The brief coda with which the film ends is very hard on them. The farmer on whose land they're eventually allowed to camp, chats up a farm girl in a somewhat desultory manner. Inviting her for a roll in the hay, he acknowledges that actually there's no hay to roll in, just 'forty quid's worth of lousy old wheatstraw' and a few 'fertilizer bags, all plastic'. If this weren't sign enough that the Pratts' rural idyll is illusory, when Keith suggests that wind blowing through the strings of Candice Marie's guitar is making a sound 'in harmony with the birds', there's an immediate cut to the inside of the chicken battery with the birds squawking in misery. And, in the final shots, as Candice Marie drones out another conservationist anthem, criticising the twentieth century's disposable treatment of humanity, Keith crawls through a barbed wire fence to defaecate among the menacingly advancing free range pigs in the next field: a fascist swine at home at last, presumably.

If this series of ironic counterpoints indicates that there's no hope for Keith and Candice Marie, the film is not at all bleak in its conclusions. The society from which they've cut themselves off is a great deal more fun than they'll ever be. The Dorset characters will carry on failing to conform to the country yokel stereotype and Ray, Honky and Finger, who do get on well, will have a few pints and few laughs together before the holiday's over. What makes the other campsite characters so admirable in comparison with Keith and Candice Marie is their total lack of pretention and their quite spontaneous pleasure in ordinary or little things. While Keith pompously congratulates himself on finding somewhere to pitch his tent among 'the *endymion non-scriptus*', Finger's similar delight is expressed more immediately, 'Hey, look at them bleedin' bluebells, bleeding millions of 'em.' In one sequence Ray, Honky and Finger spend the evening down at the local pub enjoying a friendly game of darts. Meanwhile tucked up in their sleeping bags, Candice Marie plays with Prudence, her kitten shaped hot water bottle, and Keith reads *The Guinness Book of Records*. The film seems to ask, 'Well, who would you rather pass the time with?' When Finger and Honky invite Ray to get the bus down to Swanage to join them there for the day, it's a genuine and direct gesture of friendliness which gleams like a nugget in the context of the Pratts' complacent do-gooding and self-satisfied hypocrisy.

On the one hand we have people who simply get on with their lives and have a good time in an open, unselfconscious way, and on the other we have the Pratts and their deadly system. Leigh's concern with the human scale is nowhere clearer than it is in *Nuts in May,* his point of view nowhere more explicit. But for all this *Nuts in May* is not a simple film. Although the perspective is certainly satirical – Keith and Candice Marie are indeed Pratts with all that that entails – our judgments cannot be entirely black and white. Ray, Honky and Finger are not actually admirable characters in any pure sense, but measured against the absolute standards to which Keith and Candice Marie so ludicrously aspire, we come, first, to tolerate them and finally to understand them. Because the film is set among people on holiday, it draws on a great fund of common experience in its audience and who is there, initially, who doesn't take

Keith's side when he goes over to complain about Ray's transistor radio? We probably find Ray rude and unco-operative when he refuses to turn it off. It's only slowly, as we come to see Keith's inability to negotiate over anything on a simple human level that we understand Ray's reason for continuing to play the radio: Keith put his back up.

The first appearance of Finger and Honky is scarcely likely to endear them to many members of the audience. They're crude, noisy and uncouth. Once more, our initial sympathies might lie with Keith and Candice Marie in having to deal with yet another unruly intrusion on their peace and quiet, but when it slowly becomes clear that Honky and Finger are warm, friendly people as well, the initial judgment grows more difficult to sustain and in the final confrontation over the lighting of the fire, we're prepared to see not only that Finger is badly put upon by Keith's homiletic busy-bodying, but that he's actually the more reasonable.

Although the end of *Nuts in May* ridicules the Pratts' continuing commitment to a system which has been revealed to be palpable nonsense, Leigh is hard on them because, having been given an opportunity to take stock of themselves, they pass it up. There are moments throughout the film, when each of them almost has the audience's sympathy. Although at first Candice Marie is the one who goads Keith into complaining to Ray, she changes her mind about him and sets about breaking the ice in a much friendlier attitude. She may be pretentious and silly but her heart's in the right place. When Keith runs off into the woods in tears it's impossible to condemn him outright for all the monstrous behaviour we've seen before, because here, it seems, is a genuine catastrophe in his life and one from which he might learn. In other circumstances, the revelation to him that his philosophy is untenable could almost be tragic. The trouble with them is that they only have each other, and since we've already seen that as a marriage it's no great shakes, they're doomed, alas, to go on behaving in the same, hollow way, making fools of themselves in their relationships with other people with neither being able to do anything to help the other.

There's another side of the coin, though. They have organised their attitudes into a response to the world which is based on conscience. Although their ideals are, as I've suggested, no more than a closed system, they are ideals for all of that and the problems which beset Keith are the same problems confronting anyone who tries to impose upon the unpredictable variety of life a single system of thought. The faults in Keith's ideology are attributable to his lack of understanding of the diversity of other people's experience ('Get back to your tenements' he roars, after Finger and Honky have indulged in a spot of noisy foreplay in their tent) and his consequent intolerance. If *Nuts in May* can be reduced to a single meaning, it is an argument for tolerance.

As with Honky, Finger and Ray, there are many characters in Leigh's work who appear, initially, to be unsympathetic, even occasionally repellent, but who seem to grow into more complex people as the audience's acquantance with them increases. This happens in a fairly straightforward way in the thirty minute television play, *The Permissive Society*. Les brings his girl friend Carol back to the high-rise council flat in which he lives with his mother, step-father and sister. The sister, Yvonne, a young divorcee, is getting ready to meet a new man, Maurice. Tea is made. Les watches television and eats a piece of meat pie while sprawling across the sofa. Yvonne irons her dress, washes up with Carol's help and goes out. It's clear that throughout this action, Carol is not pleased with the way Les behaves. He makes silly jokes, doesn't hang up his clothes properly and eats the pie even though they're supposed to be going out for a meal. Yvonne's mood is buoyant as she anticipates meeting with Maurice, and Carol feels excluded from her chatting to Les about work and Les's good natured but feeble brotherly banter. Once Yvonne has gone, Carol's ill humour becomes aparent.

LES: You're in a right bad mood aren't you?
CAROL: It's hardly surprising is it? Why can't you sit at the table for your tea?
LES: What?
CAROL: Did you have to sprawl all over the furniture eating your food off the floor? And why didn't you help with the washing up? You were keen enough to get rid of Yvonne.
LES: Shut up.
CAROL: Anyone'd think you didn't want me here.
LES: Shut up.
CAROL: Don't tell me to shut up.
LES: I can't help it.
CAROL: Course you can. Nobody's forcing you to behave like that. And it's about time you learned a few manners.

It seems at this point as if there's little hope for their tentative relationship but when Les confesses that he's not really sure of how to behave with girls and apologises – 'I'm sorry about before. I always have me tea on the settee. Except at Christmas.' – Carol understands that he is, in fact, sensitive and unsure of himself. She kisses him, and at that moment Yvonne returns, having walked up all one hundred and forty steps to the flat after being stood up by Maurice. As Carol and Les prepare to go out themselves, Les suggests, 'Do you think we ought to ask her if she'd like to come. She looks right miserable.' Yvonne doesn't want to go out, though, and as Les and Carol go she's left starting into space in the kitchen

The shifts of mood in the play are the result of the characters' deeply felt responses to what happens. As Carol's perception of Les moves from resentment at his slobbishness to a deeper and fuller appreciation of his human qualities, the audience pays the price for its own judgments of Les in the earlier moments of the play. His offer to Yvonne that she joins them for the evening is an unforced act of generous and loving care, even though it counterpoints the sense of desperation there is in Yvonne's disappointment.

The play takes no sides. The perspective seems cool and objective. The characters exist. They live through the moments in their lives. They are observed. But because of the potency of the performance, through the sheer interest of watching 'real life' unfolding, the audience is compelled to care. And in caring are to be found the riches in people, whether of sadness or something better, which, we realise, Leigh finds, too. It is extraordinary that in work which is as original as Leigh's and which can so easily be identified by its own characteristics, the director's hand should be so relentlessly invisible. This is because the substance of his plays and films is not to be found at the surface of events or in the way in which he handles form, but in the lives of his people, as people. It's at this level of engagement that Leigh shows his hand. It matters that Les and Carol find each other. It matters that Yvonne is stood up. These are not events to shake the world, but at the simple human level they are things to care about, and to care is to make an action on behalf of humanity, particularly if we have had to battle through our prejudices to do so.

Leigh's ostensibly dispassionate stance is born of a commitment not to work it all out for the audience. He sets out all the elements, and allows them to emerge slowly, as indeed they would in life, leaving the audience with the task of fitting the pieces together as it may, finding that this judgment on this character was perhaps too hasty in the light of what he did here, that judgment on that event was ill considered in the light of that event there. He never plants obvious clues; nothing is romanticised, things never get sentimentalised. Working-class people for example are not salt-of-the-earth rough diamonds who speak as they find but have hearts of gold. They are particular people, living in a particular environment and shaped by a myriad of factors which make up their background. He makes life difficult for the spectator who needs a quick path to knowing who the good guys are.

The combination of his apparently cool treatment of the characters and his deliberate withholding of an instantly identifiable point of view has led to the assumption by many critics that his is essentially a voyeuristic approach. We peep through the keyholes, it is said, and are invited to sneer at what we see on the other side of the door, at the rather empty and somewhat pathetic lives of his lower-class characters. *Grown-Ups,* in particular, attracted a great deal of comment in these terms.

When Dick and Mandy, the young, poorly educated, working-class couple move to their new council house, apart from the immediate problems of setting up the first home they can call their own, they have to face the added complications of finding that they live next door to one of their old teachers and his wife, and of being visited virtually every day by Mandy's frumpish older sister, Gloria. None of these characters seems to have much going for them. Dick looks like a contemporary rendering of Neanderthal man; his wife, while young and pretty, has the cramped air of one who is already middle-aged. Gloria, all impenetrable leechlike vitality, is too thick skinned to pick up the hint that she's in the way; the two teachers have a frigid parody of a marriage in a neat sterile home where neither ever really connects with the other. The sixth character, Mandy's friend Sharon, has a dour and lugubrious outlook on life. When she's shown around the house she finds it 'filthy' and 'small', even though it has the distinction of being the last house in the row of council properties. The rest of the street, beginning with the house of Ralph and Christine Butcher, the teachers, is, as Mandy proudly points out, 'private'.

Having their own home is a big step for Dick and Mandy, and one they hardly seem equal to. Dick finds that 'the bleeding garden's in a bit of a state' and suggests concreting it over as the remedy. Mandy is full of plans for redecoration but nothing gets started. In one scene they stand in the bit of garden at the front of the house looking as out of place as two newly arrived spacemen studying the landscape of some alien planet.

The problem wth Gloria gradually becomes unbearable. She keeps 'just popping in' but invariably stays all evening and has to be walked to the bus station. She usually brings a gift of some kind, drinks for a house-warming, and, in one scene, a second hand vacuum cleaner, tokens which make it difficult for Dick and Mandy to be forceful with her. When the hints get heavier that she's not wanted she brushes them aside with the practised off-handedness learned in a lifetime of rejection. She's staking out a territory for herself. When she sees the house for the first time, she says of the spare room 'This my room is it?' and when Mandy talks about having a baby Gloria instantly offers to stay all night and babysit whenever they want her to. Her position, though, is one of desperate sadness. Dick and Mandy are eventually reduced to going out when she comes round to get rid of her, but in one sequence she even tags along here, too. Sitting in the pub with them while they persistently tell her that she's got to go home, she breaks down, and in one of the most moving scenes in all Leigh's work, reveals to the audience that it is being unloved that has made her unloveable. Throughout the film it's been clear that Gloria is driven to muscle in on

Mandy's home by her need to belong, but the inner desolation suggested by her breakdown lays open the whole of her life, a life in which the audience is now deeply entangled.

Dick's response – 'You wanna pull yourself together, gel.' – is as honest a piece of advice as a man of his limitations can give in the circumstances. Leigh sketches the society which shapes Dick: the irrelevant schooling, the emphasis in the boy's background on macho behaviour and values and the soul-destroying job of washing up in a hospital kitchen. But there are signs, too, that he's maintained some of his true nature intact. He and Mandy genuinely share their problems – far more so than the Butchers – and his sensitivity is illustrated when Gloria suggests to Mandy, as they unpack Mandy's china ornaments, that she throws away the wall plaque of an alsatian's head. Mandy doesn't much care for it either but it has to be kept because Dick's mother liked it.

When matters finally come to a head with Gloria and she's locked out of the house she runs next door to the Butchers. There follows a brilliant sequence in which, with Gloria locked in the Butchers' bathroom, Mandy, Ralph, Christine and Dick try to entice her out while Sharon hovers at the bottom of the stairs. Christine Butcher takes command, gets them all out of the way and finally manages to persuade Gloria to come downstairs. Once she's there, all but Sharon converge on her again and a rugby scrum develops on the stairs with Dick and Mandy losing their tempers. Christine again saves the day, and gets everyone out of the house, but not before, with the camera held steady on Gloria on the stairs, Sharon's head bobs into shot as she too joins in the attempt to get Gloria to leave.

Christine's presence in the film up to this point has brought to light only her whimsical behaviour in the rather arid marriage, her slightly reserved friendliness with her new neighbours and the fact that, as a teacher, she's a great deal more energetic and apparently committed than her husband. (Ralph's contempt for the kids in his RK class – of whom Dick was once one – is not even concealed.) Once she has a human situation to deal with, however, she copes better than anyone. She calms Gloria down and goes next door to sort out with the others what's to be done. Ralph hangs around in his own back garden, watching the conversation through the window. Her attempts to reconcile Dick, Mandy and Gloria are successful. A taxi is called for and Mandy and Sharon take Gloria home. Later that night when she's in bed with her husband, she says to Ralph, who's reading about dinosaurs, 'I hope there aren't any human beings in that book.' When he asks her what she means she tells him that what she wants is love, sex and and a family.

The final moments of the film move us on nine months from these events. It's almost Christmas and Mandy is expecting the arrival of her baby any day. Gloria calls, and finding the Butchers about to get into their car, exchanges a few friendly words of greeting but doesn't keep them hanging around in the cold, even though on the afternoon of the big fight on the stairs she'd done a bit of ritual territory staking by calling Christine 'Chris', taking over her knitting and quietly demanding tea and biscuits. She, it appears, has learned something from the experience. In this respect the film's ending is gently optimistic. A potentially damaging situation has been overcome and the family is still together. There's a greater tolerance of Gloria's presence and she's even about to go out and meet a man, although there is some doubt in Dick's and Mandy's minds about whether he'll turn up.

The triumph of most of the people in *Grown-Ups* is that for all their personal limitations and misplacement either at work or at home they do cope with their problems and come to a fuller understanding of each other. In achieving this they confound the audience's expectations of them. Dick and Mandy work harder at their marriage than Ralph is able to. Christine, in her way of dealing with the problem which Gloria presents, is a fuller and more compassionate person than first acquaintance suggests. And perhaps Christine has actually learned from Dick and Mandy. When she tells Ralph what her real desires are, it's in the evening of the day in which Dick has shown a loving concern for his wife; 'Look what it's doing to my missus', he says when Christine goes round to sort something out about Gloria. Only Ralph remains apparently unchanged by experience. With his irritating mannerisms and obvious inability to cope with the rough and tumble of the relationships into which he's thrust, it could be, perhaps, that he is no more than a figure of fun. Although in the scheme of the film he is the lonely isolate and not Gloria, his very exclusion from the mutual involvement of the other characters is more sad than ridiculous. But more disturbing is the sense of his being a lost soul. A teacher of Religious Knowledge he may be, but the job gives him nothing and he gives nothing to the job. His inner life appears to be at the very brink of fantasy; his obsessions are the Loch Ness Monster, dinosaurs and the unexplained, belief in which seems scrambled in his mind with religious faith. There are moments in the film when this confusion is suddenly released in moments of furious self contradiction. When Christine questions some point about the Loch Ness Monster he launches into a tirade, with 'You've got no faith, woman; Faith, Hope Charity . . .' adding flying saucers and all manner of other paranormal phenomena to the list. In another eccentric monologue he announces:

There's more life in my back garden than there is in Canterbury. Your back garden *is* Canterbury. Oh, shut up!

Like Keith Pratt, Ralph is out of touch with life.

No one is patronised in *Grown-Ups*. If anything Dick, Mandy, Gloria and Christine deserve a kind of admiration for the positive way in which they come to terms with the complexities of their mutual relationships. But it's not the unqualified admiration one might lavish on some heroic achievement. Leigh's gaze has remained fixed with equal steadiness on their competence and on their imperfections. The way in which he takes in a whole world, with 'warts and all', and his concentration on the minutiae of everyday life seem to fly in the face of many of our customary expectations of drama. Because we're so used to plays and films which obviously deal with 'issues' and present their characters in a heroic perspective, Leigh's intensely close-up look at life can take some adjusting to. A scene in which a working-class girl unpacks a box of china ornaments (which by middle-class standards epitomise bad taste) is not the sort of thing we're used to seeing on the stage or screen. So it's easier, because of habit, to see the moment as a means of deriding her than it is to engage in the task of appreciating her for the human qualities she actually possesses. Similarly, the behaviour and manners of her husband are easier to pass judgment on than are his deeply felt efforts at holding his family life together.

These aspects of Dick's and Mandy's behaviour – taste and manners – are rooted in the cultural reality of being working-class, as are their dress, language, attitudes and sensibility. They're aspects which are heightened and intensified by the film, but they are not falsified. Nor are the same features of the other working-class characters, nor indeed are the middle-class characteristics of the Butchers which are similarly heightened. Leigh's unflinching observation of the realities of class experience should not be mistaken (though it often has been) for the final word on those realities. One of the conclusions of *Grown-Ups* is that, in spite of the differences in what they know, how they speak and what they own, Dick and Mandy have a more successful marriage than Ralph and Christine, and the film compels the audience to come to terms with some of the tokens of class distinction by bringing them to an understanding of all these people for what they are.

Ecstasy, which after the success of *Abigail's Party* at the Hampstead Theatre was the next play Leigh did there, is a relentless and penetrating exploration of the lives of a group of working-class characters who don't even enjoy the prestige of a council house. Jean, a Birmingham girl living in London, pays nineteen pounds a week for a cramped and sleazy bed-sit in Kilburn. Her life consists of working in a garage as a forecourt attendant, drink and casual brutal relationships with a series of men, the latest of whom is Roy. He uses Jean for sex, but in no way cares about her. Jean's long time – and probably only – friend – is a fellow Brummie named Dawn, the wife of an Irish building labourer, Mick. Dawn's children, whom she calls 'cunts' and 'buggers', have behaviour problems. The oldest daughter, Simone, is in trouble at school.

> DAWN: 'Er's only been goin' round at school tellin' everybody 'er Daddy's died.
> Daddy's died, Jean! I says, 'I'll give you died, Simone, give you died!' . . .
> No, 'er was waitin' for me tonight, teacher at the school gates, when I went to
> pick 'em up – oh, ah: Miss Beaumont-Lewis. Said 'er was worried about Simone.
> I said, 'Oh, you're worried, am ya, worried,' I says, 'you wanna 'ave the three on
> 'em, then you'd be worried!' Said 'er was subvertive.

This is a long way from the world of *Grown-Ups.* There's no possibility here for a dialogue of any kind between the middle-class and working-class people. Miss Beaumont-Lewis is defined for Dawn by her 'wooden bleeding earrings'. She looks down on Dawn. 'She's a 'snob, 'er is'. The characters offend middle-class values at almost every turn. Dawn shoplifts from C & A and leaves her children to play in the street while she visits Jean. Her husband's behaviour alternates between sentimental indulgence of his wife and children and long nights out with drinking companions. The only character with any pretentions to gentility of any kind is Len, a friend of Mick, Dawn and Jean from a few years back who's lately returned to London, but Mick paints a picture of himself and Len in the past as 'wild fuckin' men'.

> MICK: 'Have a drink and don't give a fuck,' mm? Ah that was always the way it was
> with us, yourself and meself. . . .
> LEN: We were younger then, of course, weren't we?
> MICK: We were younger then, of course, you see? I've seen the time I could sit
> down to eighteen or twenty pints, no bother on me. That was the way it was with
> us: money on the counter, get the pints down you, and hump the fuckin'
> begrudgers!

Almost three quarters of the action of *Ecstasy* is concerned with a drinking session between these four characters after closing time when Len and Mick come back to Jean's room to mend her bed. They become progressively more drunk, they reminisce about the old days and talk about their lives now; they have a sing-song, cope with the electricity meter running out and make frequent trips to the lavatory. At the end of what has been by common consent 'a great night', a 'grand old session' and a 'lovely' time, Dawn and Mick stumble off down the road.

Left alone with Len, Jean suddenly begins to cry. To comfort her Len says, 'We've 'ad a lot to drink tonight that's all.' Jean replies:

> But I drink all the time.
> JEAN *cries throughout the following, never raising her head from her lap. And*

somewhere during this speech, LEN *starts to cry, too.*
I just sit 'ere. I didn't enjoy meself tonight. Don't want to talk about anything, just got upset. There was . . . there was a bloke 'ere earlier and em . . . Dawn was here, an', uh, 'is wife came, an' that's 'ow the bed broke . . . I don't even like 'im. I don't tell 'er anything.
Pause.
I 'ate livin' 'ere. She thinks I don't go out with anybody. An' I do. Well, I never like 'em. They don't like me, they just like 'itting me.
Pause.
I've been pregnant.
Pause.
I've always 'ad to get rid of 'em on me own.
Pause.
When she was 'avin 'ers, I was 'avin' mine. I lie to 'er all the time. I just want to die.
. . .
Just didn't think.
LEN: Eh?
JEAN: I was big 'eaded.
LEN: What about:
JEAN: I was always 'orrible to you.
JEAN *moves to the bed and lies on it, continuing to keep her face away from* LEN.
You were nice to me and, em . . . I just wanted to 'ave a good time . . . stupid.

One of the achievements of *Ecstasy* is its scrupulous evocation of the very grain and texture of the characters' lives: the squalid, freezing room with its single electric fire, the battles with landlords and posh people, the minimal expectations, the dependence on alcohol in order to wrest a good time out of anything. Another of the play's achievements is to find in these apparently hopeless and inadequate people, living at the very bottom end of society, a profound sympathy and compassion. Dawn and Mick have a kind of happiness in comparison with which Jean's life is a wilderness. Her recognition of the fact and her articulate account of herself at the end of the play is a representation of human suffering which is almost too much to bear. Jean is in a trap where her capacity to feel and thus to function as a developed individual is entirely unfulfilled by the way she lives. There is the same sense of alienation in Len. When he talks to Dawn and Mick about their marriage there is beneath his words an acknowledgment of the empty unhappiness of his own life.

Now, now, Mick, I might be footloose and fancy free, but you're a lucky man, I'd give a lot to be in your shoes – you've got a nice flat, three lovely little girls – four lovely little girls with you, Dawn, if you don't mind me saying so!
. . .
No, no, no seriously Dawn, we're 'avin' a joke now, but seriously, to see you two still together now, after all this time, so 'appy and mekkin' something of your lives, well it warms my 'eart and I just wanted to tell you that, anyway.

Len and Jean live at that threshold of life where the difference between existence and pain can scarcely be distinguished. The same is true for many of Leigh's characters. It's certainly true of Gloria and there are hints of it in Yvonne as she gazes wanly at the kitchen wall when Les and Carol are off out. What's more, for many of them there is no foreseeable end to it. Nothing short of a miracle is going to change life for the Thornleys and as we've seen miracles are not an abundant commodity in Leigh's world, even though Mrs Thornley's church sets great store by them. At the end of *Ecstasy* Len stays in Jean's flat for the night. It's transparently clear that each of them needs love, warmth and humanity. Jean goes to sleep in her bed and Len in the armchair. The audience might crave some sign that in meeting each other again they can provide the answers to each other's problems, but while the play's gaze remains fixed on them for long after they have settled down for the night, there is no suggestion that there's an easy way out for either of them. By staying with the problem rather than hinting at a solution Leigh does not allow the bubble to burst, and the audience's entanglement with the lives of Len and Jean remains with it, unresolved, after the end of the play.

One of the principal dynamics of the narrative area of Leigh's rehearsal method is to place characters in ever intensifying situations which probe the very limits of their capacity to cope. Although the material of the play or film itself does not draw its literal text from this work, the dramatic dynamic is fundamentally the same. There is no escape for his people because of who they are: the problems in which they are enmeshed derive from their nature and from the specifics of their background and past experience, not from the contrivances of plot. Jean is where she is because of who she is, and who she is has been determined by her birth, culture, class and past relationships, themselves informed by the other factors. Jean does not suffer in an existential void, her suffering is a function of her relationship with society. Herein lies a premise which can be extended to all Leigh's plays and films: that what is shown are portions of society going on, not in a generalised way, but in the actual moment to moment behaviour and relationships of real people. Part of his purpose is to lead us to question the nature of that society by involving us so deeply in the lives of the people. A happy ending, however downbeat, to *Ecstasy* would let the audience off the hook; there would be the sense that if, after all, Jean and Len can find happiness, then things can't be so bad. Things are bad, the play is saying, and here is one small and specific instance of how bad they are. Leigh offers no easily packageable answers to the problems he raises. Certainly Jean's predicament will not be relieved by a change of government. But, once again, we are urged to care, and if caring raises the inevitable questions about why life is as it is for people like Jean, then so be it. Each must look for answers in his own way.

While it is true to say that all Leigh's work embodies fundamentally the same point of view – a way of looking at society on the human scale – it would be entirely wrong to suggest that his style is unchanging. Indeed, part of the problem the critics have had . with his work is that their own expectations of what a play or film originating in improvisation *ought* to be like are constantly confounded by what his plays and films are *actually* like. Thus when Michael Billington (who on the whole is sympathetic to Leigh's work) speaks of one of the characteristics of improvisation as 'a loose and free flowing texture in performance'[5] what does he really make of Leigh's highly-wrought and burnished artefacts which might, like *Goose-Pimples* for example, look like naturalistic drama on the surface, but which, in fact, present a much more complex interplay between content and style?

In *Goose-Pimples* Jackie is a croupier in a London club. She has recently moved in as a lodger to the Dollis Hill flat of Vernon, a car salesman. Vernon is entertaining two friends for a meal at the weekend and invites Jackie to join them when she's finished work. The friends are Irving, a colleague from the car showroom, and Frankie, his wife, with whom Vernon is having an affair. Vernon's meal is a disaster as far as he's

5. *Kaleidoscope*, BBC Radio 4, 4 March 1981.

concerned because when he gets the supermarket steak out of its wrapper it's discovered to be off. Instead of eating in he takes Frankie and Irving to a steak house in Wembley. While they're out Jackie returns to the flat with Muhammad, an Arab whom she believes is into 'very big oil deals', mixing with 'other millionaires and tycoons and that'. Muhammad, on the other hand, believes himself to be in a brothel. A belief which is confirmed for him by the decor of Vernon's flat: corner bar, music-centre, a chrome and black leather sofa, swivel armchair, imitation leopardskin rugs and tigerskin wallpaper. 'You've got to admit it's me,' says Vernon proudly, unconscious of the synthesis of predatoriness and kitsch.

When Vernon, Irving and Frankie come back, Muhammad mistakes them for the barman, client and whore respectively. Since Muhammad's command of English is strictly limited, their efforts to make themselves understood are laborious and complicated. But slowly it's discovered that while Jackie is trying to pass him off as an oil tycoon for her own reflected glory, Muhammad actually works for the family business, importing livestock for Islamic sacrifice and running some shops. Simultaneously, Irving is pursuing Jackie, Frankie is after Vernon and Muhammad is trying to engage the services of both women. As the drinks flow and the hysteria mounts, Muhammad becomes the target for everyone's frustrations. Irving supplies him with laced orange juice and he throws up over Vernon's sofa. Irving accuses Vernon of having an affair with Frankie, which Vernon denies. 'Irving, I wouldn't stoop so low.' Frankie and Irving leave. Muhammad passes out on the sofa. Alone in the flat with Jackie except for the unconscious Muhammad, Vernon kisses her rapaciously and says:

> Why don't you stay with me tonight? That's your best bet. Then if he wakes up, you'll be all right.

He goes to bed. Jackie lights a cigarette and goes off to Vernon's room.

At one level *Goose-Pimples* is a parody of a West End farce. The play is in fact crafted as a farce. There's comedy of sexual intrigue, exits and entrances to off stage bedrooms and tongues and inhibitions are loosened by too much drink. There are, similarly, cases of mistaken identity and a stream of running gags flowing from them. Unlike farce, however, where the characters can endure the most buffeting physical encounters and agonies of psychological stress and yet emerge unscathed, the violence of *Goose-Pimples* is real and wounding. When, in a brief lull in the comings and goings Frankie manages to find Vernon alone, she upbraids him with her suspicion that he has another woman. We already know this to be the case, but he denies it with cloyingly fake sincerity:

> VERNON: You do believe me don't you Frankie? I wouldn't lie to you, you know that don't you? Trust me, Frankie. You do trust me, don't you?
> FRANKIE: Of course I trust you, Vernon.
> *They kiss. They're standing behind the sofa.*

At that moment Muhammad, Jackie and Irving come back into the room. It's a moment which, in conventional farce, would see the lovers springing apart, smoothing themselves down with affected nonchalance trying to appear as though nothing was happening. In *Goose-Pimples,* 'Vernon immediately terminates the embrace by dropping her backwards over the sofa'.

> VERNON: For Christ's sake, Frankie! Mind the bloody sofa.
> IRVING: What are you doing?
> VERNON: She's sitting on the back of the sofa and goes arse over tip.

FRANKIE *has rushed into the kitchen.*
VERNON: God Almighty! I wouldn't let her drive you home, Irving.
IRVING: What d'you mean?
VERNON: She's had too much to drink. She's drunk.

For Frankie, the comedy of sexual intrigue results in her degradation. The same is true for Jackie; the sexual attacks from Irving and Muhammad (and eventually from Vernon as well) are the product of her being treated as nothing more than the property of the men. It's possible at least to understand why Muhammad behaves as he does, because of where he thinks himself to be, but the parallels between his treatment of the women and the other men's, who do not labour under the same illusion, hardly require comment.

The theme of mistaken identity extends far beyond the immediate humour of Muhammad's being off course in his identification of the social roles of the others. In Jackie's increasingly desperate desire to have him seem something that he's not is a manifestation of her own urge to appear other than what she is. Frankie, fat and thirty, 'with a Niagara of cheap jewellery pouring down her cleavage'[6] looks like a hooker but is horrified when she's treated as one.

Beneath the surface of the action, but driving the characters to the frenzies of the evening is a relationship to society where the means of communication is the language of consumption. The play proliferates with the imagery of ownership. Vernon calls Jackie 'my lodger'; Muhammad wants to buy her. In one scene he releases a veritable blizzard of five pound notes in order to have her dance for him. When Frankie appears he wants to buy her, too. When the steak is found to be off, Vernon's response is a consumerist cadenza which points to the play's linked treatment of ownership, money, consumption and violence.

> I'm going to report those bastards to the area health authority. I'll take them to court. One mouthful of this garbage and we could've all gone down with food poisoning, could've bloody killed us. I'll sue those sods for every penny they've got. I'll get them closed down if it's the last thing I do.
> *During this he takes an electronic calculator from his case.*
> It's not as if you don't have to pay for it. It cost a bloody fortune. Look at this; two pounds four pence; two pounds seven pence;
> IRVING: One ninety-eight.
> VERNON: God Almighty! Six pounds nine pence! You spend six pounds nine pence and what d'you end up with? Putrified bloody horse meat!
> . . .
> I'm going to take this in Monday morning, and ram it down that bastard's throat. He won't know what's bloody hit him. I'll stuff it up his backside. I've had trouble with that sod before.

Vernon's outburst triggers a similar response in Irving and Frankie and they run through an inventory of damaged furniture, lethal hairdryers ('nearly blew her ear off') and defective washing machines. Yet it is through such possessions that they express their status to each other: cars, holidays in Ibiza, music centres. Their identities seem to reside in what they own, even though much of what they possess appears, like the clothes that Frankie buys, 'to fall apart after five minutes'.

The need to possess and consume in order to display status inevitably spills over into their relationships. Vernon gropes Frankie crudely whenever Irving's back is

6. Peter Kemp, *Times Literary Supplement*, 20 March 1981.

turned. Though she may remonstrate with 'I don't know how you can do that, Ver.' she responds to him with the same greed and rapacity with which, we learn, she laid into her dinner at Wembley.

> . . . prawn cocktails with roll and butter . . . seven different types of salad from the salad bar . . . all with Thousand Island Dressing; then there was cheesecake, and cheese and biscuits – three different kinds of cheese; coffee with cream, in a goblet; brandy; bottles of wine; not to mention the aperitifs to kick off with.

Not to mention, either, that these were the accompaniments to the main meal of 'T-bone steaks with garnish; french fries, peas, grilled tomatoes . . .'

For Irving, memorably characterised by Paul Jesson in Leigh's production, with his hands working deep in his pockets for most of the time, all relationships between men and women have been boiled down to the level of a dirty joke. The whole world, it seems, is perceived as material for the *double entendre*.

> Here, Vernon; do you know how to buy a melon in the greengrocer's? You have to give it a squeeze to see if it's ripe; you push the end in with your finger, and if it gives just a little bit, you know it's ready.
> VERNON *and* IRVING *laugh uproariously.*

Later, when Vernon mentions that the parking spaces available at his block mean he has no trouble parking his car, Irving retorts, 'No, nor do I – I'll fit into any space, eh? The tighter the better!' His sexual coarseness informs his behaviour in the play, as he pads around after Jackie, touching and nudging her at every possible opportunity. With his attention permanently fixed on his genitals, he likes to present himself as a rascally Lothario, but in reality his sexual banter is tedious and banal, his bravado, merely prurience. This ambivalence is expressed most clearly in his relationship with his wife. 'She's mine' he repeatedly tells Muhammad, seizing Frankie's wrist in a gesture of possessiveness, but when he's caught trying to fumble Jackie he rounds on Frankie, who's propping up the by now virtually unconscious Muhammad, and abuses her in terms of sexual loathing,

> IRVING: You slut! You cow!
> FRANKIE: Jesus Christ, Irving, stop it for God's sake!
> IRVING: WHY DON'T YOU JUST SUCK HIM OFF, EH?
> FRANKIE: OH FOR CHRIST'S SAKE, IRVING, DON'T BE SO DISGUSTING!
> IRVING: GO ON – GET INSIDE HIS TROUSERS! – WE ALL KNOW WHAT YOU'RE AFTER – WHY DON'T YOU JUST GET ON WITH IT?

Like the other characters in *Goose-Pimples,* with the exception of Muhammad, Irving uses other people to project upon the world the image of who he would like to be. In order for the audience to understand this, there has to be some means of identifying who they actually are, and it's here that the depth of the characterisations serves the audience very directly.

We can read Frankie at one level as the loud, brassy person she seems to be, obsessed, like everyone else, with the toys of status, and unpleasant with it. But the play shows enough of her vulnerability for the audience to get the sense of a quite different person underneath. With the discovery of the rotten steak, she's very quick off the mark in trying to redeem the evening for Vernon. She dashes out into the kitchen 'to whip something up – it won't take me five minutes . . . Sit back, relax, enjoy yourselves . . . I'm going to make a vegetable gratin.' Her offer isn't appreciated by the men. 'I don't want vegetables, I WANT MEAT.' roars Vernon, and her husband rasps, 'What's the matter with you? It's a free meal.' Her need to be appreciated and loved is obviously not satisfied by her husband, but it shows itself repeatedly in a number of ways. She is so easily mollified by Vernon's 'Trust me, Frankie' that the pathos of her situation is evident. There's more than a hint of frustrated maternalism in the way she treats Muhammad. She indulges him as a child or a pet, bringing him melon and tapping on the bowl, calling, 'Come on. Come on and have your melon – come on!' Taken in by Jackie's apparent sophistication, Frankie is anxious to impress as an habitué of the West End clubs, but when Jackie asks, 'What sort of clubs do you go to then?' the best Frankie can muster is 'Different ones.' When a little later, Jackie, in full flood, expatiates on the possibilities of her job –

> I might go to Miami and the Bahamas an' that, go on the QE2, ah, it's everybody's dream to work on that boat, you know, it's lovely.

– Frankie, completely out of her depth yet desperate to appear knowing, offers the helpful advice, 'You'll have to get innoculated.'

Frankie's real needs are personal and uncomplicated, but she's bought the flash and ersatz chic of the consumption ethic lock, stock and barrel and, in doing so, has lost herself. The audience may squirm with embarrassment at her vulgarity and tactlessness and be revolted by her lack of restraint, but it's impossible not to be touched by her vulnerability and frustration.

The kind of person Jackie wants to be is tough, ruthless and materialistic: a hard headed realist who knows the way of the world and has a shrewd eye for the main chance. Her jargon is all of 'business', 'deals', 'selling' and 'big money'. She projects herself into a brutal economic reality where 'it don't pay to get too involved' with people. If you want to do business you look people in the eye and say exactly what's on your mind.

> You've got to be straight with people, you know? Especially if there's a lot of big money changing hands. It's only good business sense in the long run.

It's a world of 'status cars' where it's important that you 'look a bit special, you know, a cut above the rest' no matter what the circumstances.

> It's worth spendin' a few grand on a really good fur coat you know . . . Shows you've got money and money talks . . . My mum always 'ad a fur coat, she 'ad this lovely astrakhan, my mum's funeral, my auntie come down from Birmingham, she 'ad this lovely short grey fur jacket on, you know, it looked really special, really glamorous.

Admirable as the idea of being 'straight with people' might be, it's not something which Jackie can actually pull off. When the mistake with Muhammad is revealed she cannot at first accept it; if there's been a misunderstanding it's because "e don't know the words in English'. But when it's clear that there is no misunderstanding, that Muhammad really does import camels, sheep and goats instead of negotiating in ships and oil, she's deeply upset. The next time he comes after her she pushes him away so hard that's he's sent reeling across the room. James Fenton, responding to a fellow critic's complaint that Leigh filled his actors with 'hatred' of their characters, offered a penetrating analysis of Jackie's character. She is, he says

> . . . torn between her intense desire for money and her perfectly genuine sexual fear of the Arab . . . The terror she knows that [he] might not be the oil sheikh she has

imagined, her brave attempts to reconcile a cosmopolitan with a distinctly suburban conception of morality, her inability to get what she wants and to be the kind of person she would respect – well, if such perceptions derive from hatred, then hatred cannot be too bad a thing.[7]

The central point here is, as Fenton implies, that it is possible to understand both what Jackie wants to be seen as, and what she actually is – a suburban lass out to impress. The wreckage of evening reduces her to the status of those commodities she's been so anxious to suggest she understands.

Even Vernon, sleek and predatory and the least sympathetic of the *Goose-Pimples* characters, shows a part of himself which doesn't square with the person he projects. He manipulates people cruelly and is patently hypocritical and unfeeling. He is, however, 'deeply ashamed' at the affair of the steak, a reaction which is understood more fully in the light of his to-ing and fro-ing with apron, dustpan and brush and rubber gloves, to empty the ashtrays or, at the end, wipe up Muhammad's vomit. Vernon's house-proudness borders on neurosis. If, as he says, his flat is him, it speaks volumes about him. It has to look immaculate but for all its flash, there's an unlived in sterility about the place, for all its gadgets it's not a home. It seems more to be the lair of some creature for whom the untidiness of life would be a violent affront. Though he lives in a style which Irving finds enviable, it's a way of life in which he never gets his hands dirty by entering fully into any kind of relationship. By the end of *Goose-Pimples* he appears to have four women on the go, one of whom, Maggie, can't be at the dinner party because 'she's taking her kiddy down to see his Dad' in Swindon. 'That's a bit of a drag for her, innit?' asks Jackie. 'Suppose so,' replies Vernon, 'It's not my problem.' Jackie's response is predictable but it suits Vernon: 'No, that's right. It don't pay to get too involved.' With Vernon, having settled for shallowness doesn't seem to have cost him any self-respect. He is not a vulnerable character and in moral chaos of *Goose-Pimples* he demolishes the final rules of farce by coming out on top. The play's judgment on him is that he is repellent, but it also asks what kind of person Vernon must be to want to come out on top of that particular heap.

Although these characters are as deeply motivated and real as any Leigh has developed, reference to a couple of the reviews of the Hampstead production will convey something of the flavour of how they appeared in performance. Peter Kemp describes Marion Bailey's Jackie in terms of her 'dainty vulgarity', her 'desperately genteel contortions of vowel and body, and a way of crossing the room in a flurry of nail biting and nervy hair-flicking that implies a rapist behind every chair'.[8] Benedict Nightingale describes her as 'mincing' and as 'speaking in a snobby-slummy accent, itself the result of some unnatural coupling between Penge and the North Circular Road'.[9] Of Paul Jesson's Irving, Kemp notes his 'jerking with laughter at his own saloon-bar smut' and Nightingale says, 'he judders all over with unseemly laughter, then starts feverishly playing what at school we called pocket billiards'. Jill Baker's Frankie 'teeters in, talking prissily through her nose' (Nightingale) giving 'a zestful cartoon performance' (Kemp). Reference is made to the men's 'hacking laughter' (Kemp) and Vernon's – Jim Broadbent – 'adenoidal conversation' (Nightingale).

It should be clear from this that while it dealt with the affairs of characters who were

7. *Sunday Times*, 29 March 1981.

8. Peter Kemp, *op. cit.*

9. *New Statesman*, 13 March 1981.

three dimensional and rounded creations, *Goose-Pimples* in its surface texture was not naturalistic. It went in what Leigh has described as 'the direction of heightened caricature', which is only to say that, at one level, the characterisations were distorted and the situation heightened.

Reference has already been made to Leigh's distillation of character in order to capture the essence of personality. In the case of *Goose-Pimples,* and to a lesser degree in *Abigail's Party* and *Who's Who,* the distillation takes us into the grotesque. Even the characters' surnames echo the butchery of the play – Gammon, Scragg (Jackie) and Staines (Vernon). The real world and the real problems of *Goose-Pimples* are deliberately presented in this distorted and heightened way in order that we may see them more clearly. This grotesque evening in Dollis Hill is a metaphor for the grotesque world we live in and the way we live it. What would you expect, the plays asks, of a rapacious, devouring society, other than to find that people in it reflect those values in their relationships with each other, rather than the values of common care, decency and humanity? Though the play's means are comic, and the final perspective compassionate, Leigh's expression is one of moral outrage. *Goose-Pimples* is a searching analysis of contemporary racism and demands a hard look at the society we have made on the level at which we know ourselves and relate to each other.

At the centre of the maelstrom sits Muhammad, finding no reason in anyone's behaviour or appearance to question the premise on which his evening with Jackie is based, and dumbfounded that the single gratification he requires is so long in coming. Meanwhile, virtually mute and certainly uncomprehending, he is misunderstood, reviled and abused – 'sambo', 'wog', 'filthy Arab' are just a few of the insults Vernon and Irving hurl at him. At the centre of a similar storm in *Abigail's Party* sits Susan, the middle- class divorcee, consumed with anxiety about what her teenage daughter's getting up to at the eponymous celebration two doors away, yet unable to communicate with her neighbours. In *Babies Grow Old* the doctors argue away esoterically while in the same room are the casualties and patients on whom their care should be lavished. Mr Payne, the rat-catcher in *Too Much of a Good Thing,* entertains in his own home the rat who's plotting the seduction of his daughter. Leigh's 'eternal fascination' with 'seeing two quite separate worlds happening in relation to each other' serves often as a means of dramatic counterpoint. It's not quite as simple as saying that, in *Abigail's Party* for example, we see Laurence, Beverly, Angela and Tony through Sue's eyes, because we don't. We see all five of them through Leigh's eyes. But the presence on stage of two separate categories of experience, creates a tension which sets each into greater relief, so that familiar things appear unfamiliar. Sometimes, as in *Nuts in May, Grown-Ups* or *Hard Labour,* for example, the two worlds have a clear division in terms of social class. Viewed from the perspective of Mrs Stone, the woman for whom she cleans, Mrs Thornley's life appears to the spectator more sharply defined, as indeed does Mrs Stone's viewed from Mrs Thornley's perspective. The presentation of the two worlds occurs at its starkest in the five minute film *A Light Snack,* where in one narrative a window cleaner scrounges a sausage roll from a woman client while a parallel inter-cut, but unrelated narrative, set in a sausage roll factory, shows one worker nagging incessantly at the other about cars and football until the silent listener eventually blows up and tells him he talks too much. The only connection between these stories is sausage rolls, the points being 'that behind whatever you use or eat is some poor bugger in a factory who made it, and you never think about that'.

As well as serving to heighten the spectator's perception of the content of the play or film, in conjunction of course with the pellucid quality of the acting and the immediacy of the apparent reality, the way in which Leigh places his separate worlds together often makes up the main sinew of the dramatic construction of his plays and films. In *Who's Who,* for example, which in some ways appears to be the least satisfactory of his works in dramatic terms because the narratives overlap only marginally, the structure is created by a series of running motifs in which the attitudes and behaviour of one class are parodied in the attitudes and behaviour of the other. Alan J. Dixon, a stockbroker's clerk, is obsessed with class and breeding. His 'life', as he puts it, is a sycophantic interest in the affairs of celebrities and the upper classes whose manners and style he tries to ape in his own suburban milieu with its little rituals of sherry drinking and put-on airs and graces. His pathetic attempts to affect this social style are thrown into sharp relief by the fact that he works in an office with genuinely upper-class people. There's more breeding in his wife's pedigree cats than he's able to muster. Meanwhile, Samantha Cathcart-Walker, a guest at a dinner party attended by the ex-public schoolboys at the office, dresses in a couturier version of punk and affects to espouse its values in the context of a conversation which has ranged over shooting holidays in Norfolk, ski-ing in Europe and the correct seating plans for dinner tables. Alan, too, is planning a holiday and discusses it with his wife at the dinner table.

ALAN: Have you been to the travel agent today, April?
APRIL: No, Alan, I forgot.
ALAN: Well, Mummo's set her heart on it. She'll be very disappointed.
APRIL: I don't know what to ask for, Alan.
ALAN: Look, you say, 'My husband and I wish to tour Balmoral, Sandringham and Windsor with my mother-in-law during the last week of August and the first week of September. Will you kindly make the appropriate hotel and coach reservations?'
APRIL: I'm not going on a coach, Alan.
ALAN: Well, me and Mummo are going on the dratted coach.

Intercut with this conversation is a scene between Francis, Alan's employer, and a private client, Lord Crouchurst: 'a charming man' according to Alan, 'He once asked me the way to the office toilet.' Lord Crouchurst ('family motto, Wealth is Strength') is making plans for his mother, too. 'She's extremely well. Bit low on funds . . . she's down to something like her last fifty thousand.'

In another of the film's echoes, Alan's obsession with appearances, status and order is shared by one of the boys, Nigel Carlisle. With Alan it's expressed in his collecting the autographs of the famous, reading Debrett's and making wall charts of the state hierarchy which he calls 'Alan Dixon's Tree of Great Britain'. With Nigel, the obsessions are more mundane. He doesn't like his flatmate's shoes on the sofa or his habit of not cleaning the bath and when, at the dinner party, it's revealed to the guests that the soup he's prepared is from a tin, he's mortified. The total of their lives is similar, too. Dixon's pretentions stifle any opportunities he has for making real relationships. His marriage is empty and in casual acquaintance he bores people to death. Living in his own fantasy, his engagement with the real world is one of failed connections. The killjoy Nigel actually inhabits the substantial reality on which Dixon's fantasies feed, but his preoccupation with superficial displays of decorum lead to his failure to connect with Samantha, with whom he appears to be having some kind of tentative relationship. In the deftness of the cross-referencing between one world and the other, and in the comic inversions of behaviour, sets of values and actual events, *Who's Who* has its dynamic and its strength.

In the making of *Who's Who* because the particular world of the upper-class characters took so long to investigate, Leigh ran out of time. A great deal of pre-rehearsal was consumed in simulating the running of a stockbroker's office so that the actors could play characters who understood its working with complete conviction. The interlocking network of relationships which constitutes the old boy system had also to be thoroughly explored. When the dinner party guests talk about the off-screen characters who are part of their common acquaintance – 'David . . . Richard . . . Stephen and Amanda . . .' these are not simply names plucked out of a hat, but elements of real substance in the on-screen characters' lives. Because of the complexity of this background work, Leigh didn't have time to develop the narrative he wanted to, and was left at the end of pre-rehearsal with a number of separate balls to keep in the air simultaneously. This possibly accounts for why the construction of *Who's Who* yields itself rather more easily to analysis than the construction of most of his other work.

For it is the case that with most of the other plays and films it is extremely difficult to see exactly how they work. Life does appear, on the surface, just to stream along, with no obvious signposts of conventional plot structure to hold the narrative together. The principal dynamic, of course, has already been discussed. Leigh's plays and films engage the audience in a world which is apparently real, then deepen that engagement by making the audience's perception of the characters more and more complex. These perceptions are further heightened by his setting within the same frame aspects of life which alienate each other.[10] The basis of this method of construction is not the progress of a linear narrative but the interlacing of a number of inner tensions.

In one of the five minute films, *Old Chums,* for example, Brian, a young man with his legs in irons, sets off to go to the pictures one afternoon but runs into Terry, a friend from the past. The action of the film covers the few minutes it takes for Brian to get from his own front door to the car park and into his invalid car, during which he's off-handedly hindered by Terry's affable, boasting reminiscences. On the surface, the film really does seem to be no more than a slice of life, showing only the brief meeting of a couple of blokes who used to knock around together. The action is unspectacular and the setting, a nondescript modern council estate, unremarkable. But the film, for all that it's tiny in scale and jokey in tone, is unsettling because of the tension between the separate experiences of the two men and how this affects their view of the present. Terry's conversation is the stuff of man-to-man pub talk: cars, sex and the odd punch up. In one telling gesture he luxuriously scratches his belly while making an inventory of his past sexual conquests. Brian, sitting in the narrow, cramped confines of the invalid car, turns away. While Terry reflects warmly on common past acquaintances, the memory of them is altogether sharper for Brian. Terry's recollection of the adventures of one Frankie Paine, a bit of a lad by Terry's account, holds no pleasure for Brian: 'I saw him the other day. Driving like a madman in Fenchurch Street. He wants to grow up, that bloke.' If the past is something they shared, a common enjoyment of it is now impossible. Terry, physically robust and

10. I use the word 'alienate' here, overworked as it is by the Brecht industry, in the sense of 'to make strange'. For a full discussion of this meaning see Needle and Thompson *op. cit.*, *ch.6*, a clear and unfussy analysis.

gregarious, sociable and well-meaning in his ease, brings only pain to Brian for whom all movement is a struggle, who lives with his mother and goes on his own to the pictures in the afternoon. It would be supremely foolish to endow *Old Chums* with too much significance. By virtue of its length alone it can only be lightweight, but it sounds themes which would usually be associated with more substantial works of art. It's about the casual damage of human relationships – Terry wounds Brian simply by being himself – about time and the sadness of change. The final shot of Brian driving off among the flats while Terry saunters into frame is gently chilling.

When Jackie first brings Muhammad to the flat in *Goose-Pimples,* the misunderstandings between them are hilarious. She shows him, for example, a brooch in the form of a cluster of cherries which he tries to eat. When she stops him, he pockets it thinking it's a gift. But later in the play, as Muhammad tries to ring for a taxi without the least idea of how English telephones work, Vernon and Irving draw up their chairs like an audience to watch his hopeless attempts. Vernon laughs once, then again and finally laughs once more. By the time he's finished any humour has long since died; the laughter's roots in cruelty are exposed, bringing back uneasy echoes of the audience's laughter from earlier on. In *Ecstasy* there is a source of tension in the gulf between Jean's social behaviour and her inner desolation: she can function as a friend with Dawn, but lies 'to her all the time'. The almost palpable presence of Dawn's children in the play – although they're never seen – assumes a new significance when we learn of Jean's abortions.

To this complex interconnecting mesh of ideas and echoes, themes and responses which make up the inner tensions of Leigh's plays and films, there has to be added what is probably his greatest talent of all: his ability to distil to their very essence the moments in the lives of his characters. In *Home Sweet Home* for example, the social worker, Melody Henderson, bullies Stan into having his thirteen-year-old daughter, Tina, home for the weekend. Tina's been in care since Stan's wife left them, but he's only been to see her 'four times in the last year'. In the scruffy back garden of his house Stan watches Tina aimlessly kicking at a paving stone on the lawn.

STAN: Here. You remember the time you got lost? Eh?
TINA *looks round.*
    Me and your grandad couldn't find you.
TINA: When was that?
STAN: When you were a kid. Gone for hours.
    TINA *crosses towards shed.*
    Here. We'll get a bit of dinner off my mate tomorrow. Yeh? A geezer I work with – his missus says she'll cook us a bit of dinner. Yeh?
    By now TINA *has wandered near* STAN *and is swishing a bit of plastic wire about.*
TINA: Yes.
STAN: You were hiding in this corner.
    TINA *looks.*
    A great big rusty old television aerial you'd picked up somewhere. Remember?
TINA: No.
STAN: Yeh. Had a load of old wire on the end of it. We took it away from you.
    You went spare.
    No response.
    Do you want me to take you to the pictures tonight, eh?
TINA: Yes.

STAN: Get something to eat, eh?
TINA: Yes. (*Pause.*) It wasn't a television aerial.
STAN: What?
TINA: I thought it was a curtain rail.
  TINA *is still swishing about with her plastic wire.* STAN *watches her.*
STAN: Don't do that. Come on.
  STAN *goes away inside.* TINA *remains and goes on swishing.*

In this entire scene there is only one exchange which is related to the present moment – 'Don't do that. Come on.' The rest is all about some other time – 'when you were a kid', 'tomorrow', 'tonight'. The essence of the scene is that there is no substance to the time-present of these two people and yet that is where they exist, with her swishing aimlessly and him trying to recall the past or generate some enthusiasm for the future. Firmly fixed in a real place and in real behaviour, the scene evokes effortlessly, and almost subliminally, the exact quality of this particular relationship and its evasion of what is happening now.

  This one tiny example of Leigh's gift for distillation and compression could be multiplied again and again by other examples from throughout his entire output; for it is ultimately the secret of the compelling fascination which his work possesses that he is able, through a moment, a gesture or an image, to summon up the sense of a whole world, a whole life. Reality does not stream by as we watch it, in his work, it unfolds in moments which are dense and packed with meaning. These moments are frequently almost impossible to recapture in description or analysis because they are essentially visual.[11] There is the particular atmosphere of the quiet, sunlit suburban streets in *Bleak Moments,* for example, through which Hilda, Sylvia's mentally retarded sister, walks back from the sheltered workshop; there is the incessant gum-chewing of Kay Adshead's Linda in *The Kiss of Death,* which has the quality of both a specific mannerism and a cultural activity; in *Home Sweet Home* the barrenness of Stan's afternoons is defined in his sitting alone in his house listening to Sinatra through stereo headphones. Such moments are not confined to the films. In *Abigail's Party,* the exactness of Alison Steadman's physical portrait of Beverly and Harriet Reynolds' performance of the particular quality of Susan's stricken endurance are almost impossible to redefine, but are indisputably part of the play's text.

  Although it is not an exact one, there is a parallel with the way in which Leigh's plays and films work, in the poetry of Philip Larkin. Larkin is able to turn an everyday event, caught in simple language, into a metaphor for the human condition. While the very phrase 'human condition' draws attention to itself by its grandeur, Larkin eschews any such thing. The elements of his poetry are often no more than the vocabulary and cadence of ordinary speech, a bit of scruffy suburban landscape, the closely observed behaviour of a character or two and the sense that somehow these elements combine to create something larger than the everyday surface they record. In *Afternoons,* for example, Larkin watches some 'Young mothers assemble / at swing and sandpit' on 'The new recreation ground'. 'Behind them' are their homes, 'An estateful of washing / And the albums, lettered / Our Wedding lying / Near the television'. On the recreation ground itself, in the early autumn afternoon, 'the wind / Is ruining their courting-places'. This plain suburban setting and the everyday event hold for Larkin a muted tragedy. The young mothers' 'beauty has thickened / Something is pushing them / To the side of their own lives.' The image of these young

11. Leigh is the first to acknowledge the contributions of designers and cameramen in the process through which he defines and distils the visual images in his work.

women is developed into a quiet lamentation for the passing away of time.[12] There is no straining for significance; the metaphor keeps faith with the recorded event and emerges naturally and organically from the moments which are observed. Nor are there any phoney poetics. The poem does not say, 'And As I Watched These Women I Thought, How Like Life.' There is a unity between the thing observed and its meaning which is accomplished so subtly that the shift from one to the other registers only as the smoothest change of gear in thought, occurring, in the case of this poem, on the sudden brutality of the word 'ruining'.

Leigh's eye for the telling everyday detail and his feeling for the poetic resonances of everyday situations are faculties he shares with Larkin. In offering some way of assessing the power of Leigh's work, and of identifying its significance, it seems right to suggest that he wrings from the substance of ordinary existence a concern for the quality of people's lives which is minute and passionate, but without sentimentality or simplification. It is a matter of total conviction with him that if we are to understand ourselves we must learn to look at the material conditions of the real world with rinsed eyes, to see the true measure of what life does to people. His plays and films are showing us, refracted through heightened perception and poetic sensibility, the way we live now in bitter and impersonal times.

12. *The Whitsun Weddings*, Faber and Faber, 1964.

APPENDIX

A complete checklist of all plays and films devised and directed by Mike Leigh.

THE BOX PLAY
Midlands Arts Centre for Young People, Cannon Hill, Birmingham
Performed 18 December 1965

SIDNEY	Rod Brookes
LULU	Janet Brookes
PA	Les Blair
MA	Susan Walker
BIG SISTER	Diz Marsh
LITTLE BROTHER	Cliff Smith
FIRST GIRLFRIEND	Annette Teofil
NURSE GIRLFRIEND	Lally Percy
THIRD GIRLFRIEND	April Price
PEDLAR	Steve Morris
LITTLE GIRL	Susan Jeffries
SECOND NURSE	Sandra Hand
UMBRELLA MAN	Bill Fisher
OLD SOLDIER	Mick Scully
STRANGER	Michael Flynn

Designer: Mike Leigh

MY PARENTS HAVE GONE TO CARLISLE
Midlands Arts Centre for Young People, Cannon Hill, Birmingham
Performed 13 May 1966

JANE	Jane Millward
DIZ	Diz Marsh
LINDSEY	Lindsey Armstrong
COUSIN SANDIE	Sandra Hand
SUSAN	Susan Jeffries
JANET	Janet Brookes
MIKE	Mike Truman
TREV	Trevor Savage
CLIFFORD BONE	Clifford Smith

Designer: Mike Leigh

THE LAST CRUSADE OF THE FIVE LITTLE NUNS
Midlands Arts Centre for Young People, Cannon Hill, Birmingham
Performed 2 July 1966

SISTER DUNLOP	Sandra Hand
SISTER SAMPSON	Janet Brookes
SISTER PADDY	Diz Marsh
SISTER CAPONE	Jane Millward
SISTER BOURNVILLE	Susan Jeffries
ONE MAN	Mike Truman
ONE MONKEY	Cliff Smith

Design and music: Steve Morris

NENAA
Royal Shakespeare Company, Conference Hall, Royal Shakespeare Theatre,
Stratford-upon-Avon
Performed Summer 1967

GERALD		Gerald McNally
LUIGI		Peter Rocca
DELIVERY BOY		Edward Lyon
CUSTOMERS	Louis Mahoney	Mike Billington
	Matthew Roberton	C.G. Bond
	Richard Williams	Robert Davies
	David Weston	Peter Gordon
		Roger Lloyd Pack

INDIVIDUAL FRUIT PIES
E.15 Acting School
First performance 3 July 1968

RONALD	David Atkinson
MRS McAULEY	Jane Briers
ANDY	Robert Putt
BETTY	Sarah Stephenson
MRS BRIDDON	Gwen Taylor
MARY BRENT	Peggy Goodson
GERALD SWANN	Edward Caswell

Designer: Mike Leigh

DOWN HERE AND UP THERE
Royal Court Theatre Upstairs
First performance 1 August 1968

GERALD	Gerald McNally
GUS	Robert Putt
KIT	Amaryllis Garnett
PAT	Gwen Taylor
BERT	David S. Boliver

Designer: Mike Leigh

BIG BASIL
Manchester Youth Theatre at the Lesser Free Trade Hall, Manchester
First performance 4 January 1969

BIG BASIL	Noel Sanders
HIS MUM	Elizabeth Byrne
HIS DAD	Roy Swindell
ANN, HIS SISTER	Jennifer Bratby
DAVE ASPINALL	Patrick McManus
HOOPER	Nigel Roberts
GRANGE	Alan Rose
ROBINSON	Stephen Lee
EVANS	Roy Kershaw
IAN AT THE BUS-STOP	Leigh Banks
LIZ AT THE BUS-STOP	Judy Major
SCHOOLMASTER	Steven Pimlott
HEADMASTER	Philip Bartle
YVONNE	Julia North
TURNER	Robert Cogo-Fawcett
SNOWDON	Alan Maley
ASPINALL	Christopher Wilde
TUCKSHOP LADY	Norah Forbes
GLOBETROTTER	David Waterhouse
BEATNIK	Jenny Kerwood
JANE	Kathy Richardson
OLD LADY	Francine Bramwell
FIRST SHOPPER	Bridget Philpott
SECOND SHOPPER	Irene Lowndes

CHRIS   Martin Brennan
AUNTIE ADA   Janet Payne
LINDA   Sara Browne
EWART   Alex Fraser
JUDY   Marla Goldstone
PAMELA   Helen Broughton
LYNDA   Norah Forbes
LINDSEY   Bridget Philpott

Designer: Janet Payne

EPILOGUE
Sedgley Park College/De La Salle College Joint Drama Department, Manchester
First performance 27 June 1969

FATHER BLACKBURN   Tony McGrath
FATHER McKENNA   Chris Wightman
MRS FLEET   Vee Cowlishaw
DAVE FLEET   Dave Walker
SISTER DOMINIC   Angela McHale
SISTER EUGENIE   Christine Makin
MR SOUTHWORTH   John Monk
ALAN   Martin Davis
NICK   Tony Edwards
VIVIENNE   Lorraine Darwen
KEN   Fergus Reynolds
PENITENTS   Ann-Marie Tickle   Maureen Porter
              Lol Fearon   Mo Slack
              Margaret Costigan   Harry Thomason
              Lyn-Marie Kavanagh   Antonio F. G. Moscardini
              Jim Boyle   John Snelgrove

Designers: John Coupe and Mike Leigh

GLUM VICTORIA AND THE LAD WITH SPECS
Manchester Youth Theatre in the Renold Theatre, Manchester
First Performance 5 September 1969

GLUM VICTORIA   Kathy Richardson
THE LAD WITH SPECS   Stephen Lee
NORMAN   Roy Swindell
MRS DAVIES   Beth Edwards
OUR RICK   Michael Cooper
OUR STEVE   Patrick McManus
OUR PHIL   Nigel Vey
JUDAS   Richard Sykes
JUNE THE FLUTE   Alwyn Thompson
JANET   Lynda Whittington
ROBBIE NEXT DOOR   Laurence Kenyon
ROBBIE'S MAM   Francine Bramwell
WILF   Martin Holden
MRS ANDERSON   Jennifer Bratby
PAMELA ANDERSON   Joan Lister
MR ANDERSON   Peter Edwards
LIZ   Lynda Bone
CATHY   Janet Goddard
BARBARA   Christine Hulbert
MARIA   Barbara Malpas
MARILYN   Julia North
HELEN   Barbara Narkiewicz
JENNY   Janet Sharrocks
CHERYL   Carolyn Taylor
JANE   Mary Whiteley
LOUISE   Katrina Widiner
ALISON   Cas Williamson
MISS BROUGH   Fiona Boyle
MISS PARTAKIS   Sarita Perez

THE MATHS MASTER   Robert Andrews
THE P.E. MISTRESS   Kathy Stockton
Designer: Mike Leigh

BLEAK MOMENTS
Open Space Theatre
First Performance 16 March 1970

SYLVIA   Anne Raitt
HILDA   Sarah Stephenson
PETER   Eric Allan
PAT   Joolia Cappleman
NORMAN   Mike Bradwell
Designer: Mike Leigh

BLEAK MOMENTS (feature film)
Autumn Productions/Memorial Enterprises/BFI Production Board
1971

Cast as for the stage play, with the addition of
PAT'S MOTHER   Liz Smith
NORMAN'S FRIENDS   Malcolm Smith, Donald Sumpter
SYLVIA'S BOSS   Christopher Martin
REMEDIAL TRAINEES   Linda Beckett, Sandra Bolton,
                      Stephen Churchett
SUPERVISOR   Una Brandon-Jones
WAITER   Ronald Eng
MAN IN RESTAURANT   Reg Stewart
ENTHUSIASTIC TEACHER Susan Glanville
STOUT TEACHER   Joanna Dickens
WINE MERCHANT   Christopher Leaver

Produced by Les Blair   *Film Editor:* Les Blair
Photography: Bahram Manoochehri *Designer:* Richard Rambaut
Sound: Bob Withey

A RANCID PONG
Basement Theatre, Soho
First Performance 26 July 1971

MARILYN   Joolia Cappleman
ARNOLD   Reg Stewart
Designer: Mike Leigh

HARD LABOUR
BBC TV Play for Today (film)
First Broadcast 12 March 1973

MRS THORNLEY   Liz Smith
JIM THORNLEY   Clifford Kershaw
ANN   Polly Hemingway
EDWARD   Bernard Hill
VERONICA   Alison Steadman
MRS STONE   Vanessa Harris
MR STONE   Cyril Varley
JULIE   Linda Beckett
NASEEM   Ben Kingsley
BARRY   Alan Erasmus
JUNE   Rowena Parr
MRS RIGBY   June Whitaker
MRS THORNLEY'S FRIEND Paula Tilbrook
MR SHORE   Keith Washington
TALLYMAN   Louis Raynes
GREENGROCER   Alan Gerrard
MRS RUBENS   Diana Flacks
FRANK   Patrick Durkin

DICK — Ian East
OLD MAN — Dennis Barry
PUBLICAN — Sonny Farrar
SIKH LADY — Surya Kumari
SISTER — Irene Gawne
PRIEST — Hal Jeayes

Produced by Tony Garnett
Photography: Tony Pierce-Roberts

Sound: Dick Manton
Film Editor: Christopher Rowlands

WHOLESOME GLORY
Royal Court Theatre Upstairs
First Performance 20 February ½973

CANDICE MARIE — Alison Steadman
KEITH — Roger Sloman
DENNIS — Geoffrey Hutchings

Designer: Mike Leigh

THE JAWS OF DEATH
Traverse Theatre, Edinburgh
First Performance 4 September 1973

BRENDA — Alison Steadman
HACK — Richard Ireson
THE YOUNG MAN — Adrian Shergold

Desinger: Mike Leigh

DICK WHITTINGTON AND HIS CAT
Royal Court Theatre Upstairs
First Performance 26 December 1973

DICK WHITTINGTON — Paul Copley
HIS FATHER — Philip Jackson
HIS MOTHER — Lavinia Bertram
THE CAT — Tim Stern
THE CAT'S MOTHER — Joolia Cappleman
FATHER CHRISTMAS — Peter Godfrey
MR FITZWARREN — Roger Sloman
ALICE — Lavinia Bertram
KIM — Joolia Cappleman
HER MAJESTY'S CONSTABULARY — Roger Sloman
JACKIE — Joolia Cappleman
STEPHEN — Philip Jackson
MOTORIST — Roger Sloman

Designer: Diz Marsh

BABIES GROW OLD
Royal Shakespeare Company, Other Place and ICA Theatre
First Performance 27 August 1974

MRS WENLOCK — Anne Dyson
ELAINE — Sheila Kelley
GEOFF — Eric Allan
CHARLES — Matthew Guinness
BARRY — Sidney Livingstone

Designer: Judith Bland

THE SILENT MAJORITY
Temporary Theatre Club at the Bush Theatre
First performance 24 October 1974

MR CLANCY — Stephen Bill
MRS CLANCY — Julia North
MRS DUFFY — Yvonne Gilan

Designer: Mike Leigh

THE PERMISSIVE SOCIETY
BBC TV Second City Firsts (Studio Recording)
First Broadcast 10 April 1975

LES	Bob Mason
CAROL	Veronica Roberts
YVONNE	Rachel Davies

Produced by Tara Prem
Designer: Margaret Peacock

'THE FIVE MINUTE FILMS'
BBC TV (1975)

THE BIRTH OF THE 2001 FA CUP FINAL GOALIE
First Broadcast 5 September 1982

FATHER	Richard Ireson
MOTHER	Celia Quicke

OLD CHUMS
First Broadcast 6 September 1982

BRIAN	Tim Stern
TERRY	Robert Putt

PROBATION
First Broadcast 7 September 1982

ARBLEY	Herbert Norville
SID	Bill Colville
MR DAVIES	Antony Carrick
SECRETARY	Theresa Watson
VICTORIA	Lally Percy

A LIGHT SNACK
First Broadcast 8 September 1982

MRS WHITE	Margaret Heery
WINDOW-CLEANER	Richard Griffiths
TALKER	Alan Gaunt
LISTENER	David Casey

AFTERNOON
First Broadcast 9 September 1982

THE HOSTESS	Rachel Davies
THE TEACHER	Pauline Moran
THE NEWLY-WED	Julia North

Produced by Tony Garnett
Photography: Brian Tufano
Sound: Andrew Boulton
Film Editor: Chris Lovett

NUTS IN MAY
BBC TV Play for Today (film)
First Broadcast 13 January 1976

KEITH	Roger Sloman
CANDICE MARIE	Alison Steadman
RAY	Anthony O'Donnell
HONKY	Sheila Kelley
FINGER	Stephen Bill
MISS BEALE	Richenda Carey
QUARRYMAN	Eric Allan
FARMER	Matthew Guinness
FARM GIRL	Sally Watts
POLICEMAN	Richard Ireson

Produced by David Rose
Photography: Michael Williams
Sound: John Gilbert
Film Editor: Oliver White
Designer: David Crozier

KNOCK FOR KNOCK
BBC TV Second City Firsts (Studio Recording)
First Broadcast 21 November 1976

MR BOWES	Sam Kelly
MR PURVIS	Anthony O'Donnell
MARILYN	Meryl Hampton

Produced by Tara Prem
Designer: Myles Lang

THE KISS OF DEATH
BBC TV Play for Today (film)
First Broadcast 11 January 1977

TREVOR	David Threlfall
MR GARSIDE	Clifford Kershaw
RONNIE	John Wheatley
TREVOR'S MUM	Pamela Austin
SANDRA	Angela Curran
FROGGY	Phillip Ryland
LINDA	Kay Adshead
CUSTOMER	Elizabeth Hauck
POLICEWOMAN	Karen Petrie
MR BODGER	Frank McDermott
MRS BODGER	Christine Moore
MRS BALL	Eileen Denison
CHRISTINE	Marlene Sidaway
DOCTOR	Brian Pollitt
BRIDESMAID	Elizabeth Ann Ogden

Produced by David Rose
Music: Carl Davis
Photography: Michael Williams, John Kenway
Sound: John Gilbert
Film Edtior: Oliver White
Designer: David Crozier

ABIGAIL'S PARTY
Hampstead Theatre
First Performance 18 April 1977

BEVERLY	Alison Steadman
LAURENCE	Tim Stern
ANGELA	Janine Duvitski
TONY	John Salthouse
SUSAN	Thelma Whiteley

Designer: Tanya McCallin
Costumes: Lindy Hemming

Revived 18 July 1977 with one change of cast
SUSAN   Harriet Reynolds

BBC TV Play for Today (Studio Recording)
First Broadcast 1 November 1977
Cast as for the revived stage play
Produced by Margaret Matheson

WHO'S WHO
BBC TV Play for Today (film)
First Broadcast 5 February 1979

NIGEL	Simon Chandler
GILES	Adam Norton
ALAN	Richard Kane
FRANCIS	Jeffry Wickham
SAMYA	Souad Faress
KEVIN	Philip Davis
ANTHONY	Graham Seed

APRIL	Joolia Cappleman
NANNY	Lavinia Bertram
SELINA	Francesca Martin
LORD CROUCHURST	David Neville
LADY CROUCHURST	Richenda Carey
MISS HUNT	Geraldine James
MR SHAKESPEARE	Sam Kelly
SAMANTHA	Catherine Hall
CAROLINE	Felicity Dean
COUPLE IN WINDOW	Angela Curran, Roger Hammond

Produced by Margaret Matheson
Photography: John Else
Sound: John Pritchard

Film Editor: Chris Lovett
Designer: Austen Spriggs

TOO MUCH OF A GOOD THING
BBC Radio 3 (1979)
Not Broadcast

PAMELA	Lesley Manville
GRAHAM	Philip Davis
MR PAYNE	Eric Allan

Produced by Liane Aukin
Sound: Cedric Johnson, Julian Walther
Tape Editor: David Hitchenson

ECSTASY
Hampstead Theatre
First Performance 26 September 1979

JEAN	Sheila Kelley
ROY	Ron Cook
VAL	Rachel Davies
DAWN	Julie Walters
MICK	Stephen Rea
LEN	Jim Broadbent

Designer: Alison Chitty
Costumes: Lindy Hemming

GROWN-UPS
BBC TV Playhouse (film)
First Broadcast 28 November 1980

DICK	Philip Davis
MANDY	Lesley Manville
GLORIA	Brenda Blethyn
SHARON	Janine Duvitski
CHRISTINE	Lindsay Duncan
RALPH	Sam Kelly

Produced by Louis Marks
Photography: Remi Adefarasin
Sound: John Pritchard

Film Editor: Robin Sales
Designer: Bryan Ellis

GOOSE-PIMPLES
Hampstead Theatre
First Performance 3 March 1981

VERNON	Jim Broadbent
JACKIE	Marion Bailey
IRVING	Paul Jesson
FRANKIE	Jill Baker
MUHAMMAD	Antony Sher

Designer: Caroline Beaver
Subsequently transferred to the Garrick Theatre
First Performance 29 April 1981

HOME SWEET HOME
BBC TV Play for Today (film)
First Broadcast 16 March 1982

STAN	Eric Richard
TINA	Lorraine Brunning
HAZEL	Kay Stonham
GORDON	Timothy Spall
JUNE	Su Elliott
HAROLD	Tim Barker
MELODY	Frances Barber
DAVE	Lloyd Peters
JANICE	Sheila Kelley
KELLY	Heidi Laratta
MAN IN DRESSING GOWN	Paul Jesson

Produced by Louis Marks
Music: Carl Davis
Photography: Remi Adefarasin
Sound: John Pritchard
Film Editor: Robin Sales
Designer: Bryan Ellis

Miscellaneous pieces

A MUG'S GAME
Scenes for BBC Schools Television
First Broadcast 8 March 1973

CAROL	Gillian Joyce
MARTIN	Eric Allan
STEVE	Keith Washington

Produced by Andrée Molyneux

PLAYS FOR BRITAIN – film titles
Thames Television 1976

MAN	Tim Stern
WOMAN	Theresa Watson

Produced by Barry Hanson
Music: Carl Davis

THE IMPROVISED PLAY
Rehearsals, improvisations and scenes for *Mike Leigh Making Plays*
BBC TV *Arena* documentary film
First broadcast 4 September 1982

MICK LEEMING	David Threlfall
MIRANDA BROMLEY	Alison Steadman
MERTON SAVOY	Sam Kelly

Produced by Alan Yentob
Photography: Remi Adefarasin
Sound: John Pritchard
Film Editors: Robin Sales, Charles Chabot

Publications

ABIGAIL'S PARTY
included in *Best Plays of 1977* (Elek Ltd, 1978)

ABIGAIL'S PARTY (Samuel French, 1979)

GOOSE-PIMPLES (Samuel French, 1982)

ABIGAIL'S PARTY and GOOSE-PIMPLES (Penguin Plays, 1983)

Awards

1972	BLEAK MOMENTS	Grand Prix (Golden Hugo) Chicago Film Festival
1972	BLEAK MOMENTS	Grand Prix (Golden Leopard) Locarno Film Festival
1973	Joint winner of GEORGE DEVINE AWARD	
1977	ABIGAIL'S PARTY	Alison Steadman, Best Actress, Plays & Players
1977	ABIGAIL'S PARTY	Alison Steadman, Best Actress, Evening Standard
1981	GOOSE-PIMPLES	Best Comedy, Evening Standard
1981	GOOSE PIMPLES	Best Comedy, 'Drama' Magazine, London Theatre Critics' Choice.